Open Your Hearts

Open Your Hearts

*Messages from Our Lord Jesus
and His Blessed Mother
given to Michael McColgan*

Queenship

PUBLISHING COMPANY
P.O Box 42028 Santa Barbara, CA 93140-2028
(800)647-9882 Fax: (805) 569-3274

The publisher recognizes and accepts that the final authority regarding these apparitions and messages rests with the Holy See of Rome, to whose judgement we willingly submit.

– The Publisher

About the cover: See page xi

©1995 Queenship Publishing

Library of Congress Number # 95-72818

Published by:
Queenship Publishing
P.O. Box 42028
Santa Barbara, CA 93140-2028

Printed in the United States of America

ISBN: 1-882972-62-7

Contents

To the Reader ix
About the Cover xi
Preface xiii
Jesus: Truly Present in the Blessed Sacrament xv
Foreword by Michael H. Brown xvii
Letters from the Spiritual Directors xix
The Visions xxiii
About the Locutionist xxv
Summary of the Messages and the Threefold Call of Christ xxvii
She is With Us xxxi
"I am there ... for all" xxxiii
Let Us Be Open to the Call xxxv
Dedication xxxvii
It Shall Come to Pass xxxix
What Does Our Lady Ask Us to Do? xxxxi
Messages from the Year 1989 1
Messages from the Year 1990 3
Messages from the Year 1991 31
Messages from the Year 1992 45
Messages from the Year 1993 75
Messages from the Year 1994 97
Messages from the Year 1995 107
Messages From The Blessed Virgin Mary
      On The Ten Commandments 115
The Holy Rosary 121
The Mysteries of the Rosary 121
The Creed 122
Our Father 122
Hail Mary 122
Glory Be 122
Fatima Prayer 123
Hail Holy Queen 123
Let Us Pray 123
The Divine Mercy Chaplet 123
The Chaplet of Truth 124
The Memorare 124
Prayer To Saint Michael 125
Eucharistic Prayer of Akita 125
Act of Consecration to the Immaculate Heart of Mary 125
Prayer to the Eternal High Priest 126
Laborers for the Harvest 126

Do whatever He tells you (John 2:5)

I am the Way, the Truth and the Life (John 14:6)

To the Reader

Before reading any of the contents of this book, you are asked to pray to the Holy Spirit; asking Him to enlighten you and guide you.

- No one is required to believe in private revelation (the messages and experiences concerning Michael McColgan are considered to be private revelation). Public revelation, though, must be believed in by the faithful (that is, all that is contained in Scripture and the teaching Tradition of the Church).

- It should be noted that the contents within this book have been given to us so that we may:

  - grow in our love for and relationship with the Most Holy Trinity: Father, Son and Holy Spirit.

  - that we may love and desire to participate in the Holy Sacrifice of the Altar (Mass) and receive Holy Communion.

  - that we may desire to go to Confession frequently – asking God for the forgiveness of our sins and so, grow in holiness.

  Thus, our focus should be upon:
  - God
  - Prayer
  - the Sacraments

- Private revelation is in *no way* to be placed above the importance of Scripture. You and I are urged to read and meditate on Scripture; epsecially the four Gospels, which contain the words and events of Christ's life as recorded by Matthew, Mark, Luke and John.

PICTURED ON THE FRONT COVER:
VISION OF SEPTEMBER 6, 1994, AS SEEN BY MICHAEL
McCOLGAN WHILE IN PRAYER IN THE CHAPEL

The vision lasted for approximately one minute. What follows here is a short explanation of what the vision desires to explain to us. The vision occurred on a Tuesday afternoon one week before Exposition was to begin at the Chapel where Michael was praying. Every Tuesday following September 6 there was Exposition and Adoration of the Blessed Sacrament. The vision was a forerunner of what was to follow. Our Lord throughout His message calls for us to open our hearts to love Him in this Sacrament of Love. Michael relates, "the vision began with a priest and an altar server walking up the aisle of the Chapel. When the priest arrived at the foot of the steps leading up to the altar, he knelt down as did the altar server. The priest then bowed and kissed the first step. At that moment, the Monstrance with the Eucharist inside it, the Lamb, and the blood, pouring forth as graces, appeared. The Lamb represents Our Lord Himself, Who is the Lamb of God Who comes to take away the sins of the world... the spotless (sinless) offering to God, fully redeeming us from our sins.

The Monstrance which sits upon our altars for us to adore the Eucharistic Lord, contains the Host, Which is Jesus Who is truly present: Body, Blood, Soul and Divinity in the Blessed Sacrament. This is His gift to us: that He is always with us in every Catholic Church, present in the Tabernacle. He comes to us in Holy Communion. Jesus says to us, "I am the Bread of Life" (John 6:48) and "Truly, I say to you, unless you eat the flesh of the Son of man and drink his blood, you have no life in you; he who eats my flesh and drinks my blood has eternal life, and I will raise him up on the last day." (John 6:53,54) Jesus wishes for us to open our hearts and minds to understand this and to love Him in this, the Sacrament of sacraments; the Holy Eucharist. Many today (and throughout the centuries) refuse this gift He has given us. The vision calls us to realize the tremendous value of His Real Presence in the Blessed Sacrament and the graces which flood forth from His heart, both when we receive Him in Holy Communion and when we come before Him to adore Him. The vision also calls us to understand the overwhelming importance of the Holy Sacrifice of the Mass. Jesus wants us to love the Mass.

The blood which is coming forth from the altar (from the Lamb upon the altar) represents, in the vision, the blood of the Lamb, of Jesus, which He shed for all mankind in His crucifixion on the Cross. The Mass is Jesus upon the Cross again in a unbloody manner. The blood represents both the actual blood of Christ which He shed for us and now the graces which pour forth from His most Sacred Heart at each Mass and each time we come before Him in adoration. Jesus who is truly present in the Most Blessed Sacrament, should be the center of our lives. From Him, our Lord and Savior, comes every grace. Christ wants us to understand this.

The vision of September 6, 1994 is a strong and salient reminder from Our Lord of His gift to us and of His never-ending love for us.

* Quotes taken from The Holy Bible, Revised Standard Version, Catholic Edition, Ignatius Press, San Francisco. New Testament, copyright 1946; Old Testament, copyright 1952; The Apocrypha, copyright 1957.

Open Your Hearts

The official position of the Catholic Church remains as set down by Pope Paul VI on October 14th, 1966, i.e. that in matters of private revelation, such as this, the faithful are free to promote and propagate the messages without reference to Church authority:

A) Provided that in doing so they willingly submit themselves to the ultimate official pronouncement of Holy Mother Church on the matter;
B) Provided that the content of the messages does not constitute a change of faith and morals.

This book is distributed on that basis. It is, however, worth noting the advice of Pope Urban VIII: "In cases like this, it is better to believe than not to believe, for if you believe and it is proven true, you will be happy that you have believed, because Our Holy Mother asked it. If you believe and it should be proven false, you will receive all blessings as if it had been true, because you believed it to be true."

We accept that the final authority regarding the locutions rests with the Holy See in Rome, to whose judgment we willingly submit.

We urge you to "open your heart" and to study Our Lord's and Our Lady's messages and then to seek to live them in your daily life.

We invite everyone to truly open their hearts as they read these messages; to read them slowly and to think about what Jesus and His Blessed Mother are saying to us through the messages. Our Lady invites us to **PRAY** (she asks us to try and make time for the Rosary every day to meditate on the Mysteries of the Rosary), to go to **CONFESSION** and to be aware of sin and temptation, to strive every day to be close to God, to say "yes" to God, to **DECIDE** for God in all things and at all times. Our Lady asks us to place Jesus at the center of our lives. We need to ask Jesus to fill us with His peace so that, being full of love and hope, we can bring His light to those around us. If we listen to Our Mother and follow Jesus then our lives will begin to be transformed and so will the lives of those close to us.

JESUS: TRULY PRESENT IN THE BLESSED SACRAMENT

In His first two messages to Michael, Jesus asks us to come to Him - where He waits for us in the tabernacles of our churches, truly present in the Blessed Sacrament.

Our Holy Father, **Pope John Paul II,** in many of his writings, has spoken about the overwhelming importance of the Eucharist in the life of the Church. In his first encyclical letter, *Redemptor Hominis*, **Pope John Paul II** exhorted that, "Every member of the Church, especially Bishops and Priests, must be vigilant in seeing that this Sacrament of Love shall be at the center of the life of the people of God, so that through all the manifestations of worship due it, Christ shall be given back 'Love for Love'; and truly become the life of our souls." He stated that, "Indeed the Eucharist is the ineffable Sacrament! The essential commitment and, above all, the visible grace and source of supernatural strength for the Church as the people of God are to persevere and advance constantly in Eucharistic life and Eucharistic piety and to develop spiritually in the climate of the Eucharist. With all the greater reason, then, it is not permissible for us, in thought, life, or action, to take away from this truly Most Holy Sacrament its full magnitude and its essential meaning. It is, at one and the same time, a sacrifice-sacrament, a communion sacrament, and a presence-sacrament."

Pope Paul VI states in the *Credo of the People of God* that the Blessed Sacrament **"is the 'Living Heart' of each of our churches and it is our very sweet duty to honor and adore in the Blessed Host which our eyes see, the Incarnate Word whom they cannot see, and Who, without leaving Heaven, is made present before us."**

Echoing Our Lord's words to Michael, **Pope John Paul II** states clearly in his letter, *On The Mystery and Worship of the Holy Eucharist* that, "the Church and the World have a great need of Eucharistic Adoration. Jesus waits for us in this Sacrament of Love. Let us be generous with our time in going to meet Him in adoration and in contemplation that is full of faith, and ready to make reparation for the great faults and crimes of the world. **May our adoration never cease."**

Our Lord has spoken to us before about His great desire for us to come and visit Him, to open our hearts to Him, to allow Him to heal us and fill us with His light, love and mercy. He yearns for us to come before Him — Truly present in the Eucharist. In revelations to Sr. Josefa

Menendez to whom Our Lord appeared in the first half of this century, He said, "My heart is burning with desire to attract souls to itself in order to forgive them. Still, I sit all night and watch in the tabernacle for that soul . . . fervently hoping that he/she will come to receive Me." . . . and on two other occasions Our Lord said to Sr. Josefa, "The Holy Eucharist is the invention of love; yet how few souls correspond to that love which spends and consumes itself for them!" and "... I desire that My love in the Blessed Sacrament should be the sun to enlighten every heart and the heart to reanimate every soul. This is why My words must reach them. I want all the world to recognize in the Blessed Sacrament a God of mercy and love."

These revelations have been approved by the Church through Cardinal Eugenio Pacelli, who later became Pope Pius XII. Sr. Josefa Menendez is called "the modern day St. Margaret Mary Alacoque."

Let us with love and sincerity open our hearts to Jesus, Who is truly present in the Holy Eucharist, and to the Mother of God, our Queen and Mother, the Blessed Virgin Mary.

"When we look at the Cross, we see how much Jesus loved us then. When we look at the Eucharist, we see how much Jesus loves us now. If you really want to grow in love, come back to the Eucharist, come back to Adoration. The Eucharist is the sacrament of prayer, the fountain and summit of Christian life."

– Mother Teresa

FOREWORD

Michael H. Brown
Author of *The Final Hour, Prayer of the Warrior* and
Witness: Josyp Terelya Apparitions in the USSR

The world currently finds itself in the midst of a supernatural episode. God is trying to say something to us. I have no idea how many of the claimed locutions and apparitions are authentic, but to know we're in special spiritual times, one has only to look at the evil rising around us.

Many are the visionaries who warn that the earth is about to encounter grave events or "chastisements." Only the future will say for sure. What I do know is that the greatest chastisement is already upon us: a tremendous spiritual turbulence.

Will it surprise you to know that I don't find that daunting, nor "doom and gloom," but exciting?

We have all been given a special mission in these special times, and those who are receiving messages often speak about the need for prayer and conversion. Our prayers are especially powerful at this crucial juncture in history, and to be part of such a mission is what I find both challenging and exciting.

The Immaculate Heart of Mary is soon to triumph. The great evil which casts a long dark cloud over humanity will soon be broken. And the triumph of the Immaculate Heart will be followed by the reign of the Sacred Heart — as always Mary is the forerunner of Our Savior.

What hope! There should be little doubt left that not only does God exist, but that He is watching us very closely and promises us, after the testing here on Earth, eternal reward.

Now is the time for prayer, fasting, and discernment. Now is the time of the Eucharist. Nothing is more powerful in the face of evil than the Holy Sacrifice of the Mass. If prayer and humility result from a locutionist's messages, then we know that God is drawing forth fruits and that we are moving in the proper direction.

LETTERS FROM MICHAEL'S SPIRITUAL DIRECTORS

Father Jim Sauchelli
Pastor, St. Joachim Church

I would like to take this opportunity to introduce to the reader Michael McColgan. I met Michael around two and a half years ago, when I was preparing to embark on my first journey to Medjugorje.

Mike is a deeply spiritual young man. He is a rarity if I may say so. When I characterize Mike as a rarity, this is what I mean. He is your typical young man. He is in tune with everyday living. He enjoys sports and is very sociable. He can laugh, joke and have a real good time. He also possesses that quality of closeness to God without being a religious fanatic. If you were to meet him, you would think that he is just one of the guys. He is not. I personally feel that God has chosen him for a special mission in life.

It was not long after I met him that he confided in me about what was occurring. Our Lord and Our Lady were speaking to him in a very special way. We both were very cautious in the beginning. At first I advised him to keep these messages to himself. He wrote them down and sent them for me to read. This I did. They were simple messages and a lot like the ones that the young visionaries were receiving in Medjugorje. We then decided to give them to his prayer group; they proved to be very beneficial. When you read them in this book, you will find that they are basically the Gospel messages of Our Lord. We feel that Mary is and has been, since 1846, with the La Salette message, re-emphasizing His mission to the world.

Again, both Mike and I felt that we would like another opinion, more objective than our own. We sought the advice of Fr. John McFadden who has been very involved with visionaries from around the world. Fr. McFadden concurred with our optimism.

Michael is not a person given to hysteria. He is quite a level-headed young man. He is intelligent and wise in many ways beyond his years. He also has his quirks. He gets sidetracked. Sometimes he is pre-occupied. He doesn't have a good sense of time. He is a typical young man!

When you read these locutions, I believe that you will see as I see, that the messages are simple but urgent. They are reiterations of the Gospel message in our own time. It is true, time is running out.

Apparently, Our Lady is going to many other people to make it quite clear that now is the time to change our lives, to pray, to repent and to convert. There is a real battle going on for our souls and Mary means to pull out every stop to win us back to her Son. The messages are positive. They are not dooms-day messages. If you take the time not only to read the messages but also to live them, then the peace of Christ, that Our Lady has brought, will begin to fill your life and, through you, the lives of those around you.

Father John McFadden
Pastor, Presentation of the Blessed Virgin Mary Church

By God's mercy and in the Love of Our Blessed Mother, I have found myself to be the blessed recipient of many of the contemporary private revelations of Our Lord and Our Lady.

In virtue of my long identity with Medjugorje (nine years) and my association with renowned Mariologists such as Msgr. René Laurentin, Father Michael O'Carroll and Father Gerard McGinnity, Our Lady has led me into an ever deepening desire to spread her messages of purification, conversion and faith in her Son. To this purpose, I speak, at least monthly, at local churches, national conferences and Rosary conferences.

Coming from this blessed experience, I have prayerfully and studiously read the private revelations that are being given to Michael McColgan. Knowing Michael as I do, I am impressed by his commitment to serve the Lord as he demonstrates in every aspect of his life. This is especially true in Michael's Pro-Life activism. I find him to be a very well-balanced young man in that he is intelligent, personable and humble. Finally, let me state that I have consistently found Michael's reported locutions to be aligned with our Catholic Faith and Sacred Scripture. Also, the messages that Michael has been receiving are consistent and collaborative of other creditable private revelations that I have been reviewing. My sense is that Michael's experience is authentically supernatural.

Father Glenn Hartman
Parochial Vicar, St. Peter Church

I first met Michael in the confessional prior to Mass on Divine Mercy Sunday, 1993 — the day on which Sister Faustina Kowalska was beatified by Pope John Paul II.

While reserving all judgment on private inner locutions and visions to the ultimate discernment and pronouncement of Holy Mother the Church, I personally find nothing in the following messages which is contrary to our revealed Catholic faith.

In addition to the fact that the messages are essentially in concord with the message of Fatima and with sound Catholic tradition, there are two pertinent fruits stemming from the messages and Michael's experiences which I would emphasize.

Mary's role in the economy of salvation and our devotion to her, that is to say, her life and apparitions and our response to her, respectively, are never ends in themselves. She always leads us to her Divine Son. This is clearly the case with Michael. Both in the messages and in the events in his life one finds a strong progression from Mary to Jesus. Michael's tremendous love for Our Lord in the Holy Eucharist and his zeal in promoting Perpetual Adoration are not only consonant with the highest of Catholic piety, but also, in his case, direct fruits of his relationship with Mary.

The second flowering which, in my opinion, lends credence to the authenticity of these messages and Michael's experience, lies in his ever-increasing concern for his preborn brothers and sisters. This development in Michael of a strong pro-life regard and an ever increasing zeal for prayer and action in this apostolate for life can directly be attributed to his relationship with the Mother of Life and the messages which have also come to him from, we believe, the Heart of Jesus.

I invite the reader, then, to be open to the love of Our Lady which comes through in these messages. Take to heart the words of Our Lord contained herein. While we necessarily remain docile to the guidance of the Church — "Be children of the Church,": Saint Elizabeth Ann Seton's last words — we are thankful for these, and any inspirations, which can serve to lead us closer to Our Lord through His Mother. We join in prayer with and for Michael and remember that "There is one Spirit, but many gifts."

THE VISIONS

The locutions began in August of 1989 when Michael was 19 years old and they have continued until the present.

Michael has had visions of Our Lord and of the Blessed Mother.

Michael has seen the Blessed Mother numerous times. The first time it occurred shortly after the locutions began, in the Fall of 1989.

In the first vision of the Blessed Mother, she came wearing only a rough, white cloth garment — her hair was straight and long — very simple looking. She seemed to be in a room made of a stucco-like material. Bright rays were descending upon the wall behind her, lighting up the room. Michael said he understood that she was about 15.

Michael has found a picture that looks almost exactly like the Blessed Mother (how he saw her, the first time.) He never thought he would see the picture again after he first saw it. Four months later, it was found in the basement of a rectory where he was working. Michael asked the priest if he could have it and sure enough, the priest said yes.

He then saw her on separate occasions three other times between the beginning of 1990 and the end of 1991. In these last three visions Our Lady came looking exactly the same. Under the title **"Mother of All Mankind"** — she had a white gown and a white mantle, which Michael said "seemed to be filled with light." Her hair was black; tucked in on the left side of her mantle but on the right her hair hung in thick curls down close to the middle of her neck. Michael said that she held a Rosary (pearlish/silver) in her right hand which was long enough that it hung down past her knees. She had only a slight smile on her face and seemed to be between 18 and 21 years old. Michael said there is nothing on this earth that can compare to her beauty. Her beauty, he says, is "pure love ... that is why she is beautiful ... it is not of this world."

The visions of Our Lord began on the Tuesday after Easter Sunday 1992. During the Sorrowful Mysteries Michael saw Our Lord's face bowed, with the Crown of Thorns and blood covering His face. Jesus spoke saying, "Offer My Holy Face to the Father in atonement for the sins of all mankind."

In May of 1992, Michael had another vision of Jesus. He saw Our Lord standing before him with his arms outstretched and His heart bursting forth from His chest. In his heart Michael could feel Our Lord repeating with love, "Come to My mercy."

During the Summer of 1992, Michael continued to have visions of the Holy Face of Jesus. In August of 1992, on two occasions Michael saw Our Lord's face, His head crowned with thorns, and blood streaming down his face from the wounds - and behind Our Lord's head was a large Host as bright as the sun, with rays of white light streaming out around Jesus' head in all directions.

In January of 1993, Michael again had a vision of Our Lord, which Michael said is the most moving of all of them. He saw Jesus wearing a white garment (from His stomach upwards) with a deep red cloak around Him. Our Lord was pointing to His heart which was surrounded and pierced with thorns, with His other arm raised in a sign of peace. Flames were within Our Lord's heart and rose up out of it, as if consuming His heart. Michael said he understood this fire to represent His burning love for souls. Then during this vision a Host appeared in front of Jesus' heart. It was glowing, pure white, and Michael said he could see through the Eucharist to Our Lord's heart and understood then, overwhelmingly, that the Eucharist is our greatest means of reaching the Heart of Jesus. Michael said that this vision so moved him that it still fills him with great emotion when he meditates on the gift which Our Lord allowed him to see and understand.

Other visions have occurred and are explained in detail later in the book.

ABOUT THE LOCUTIONIST

The following "brief" is to help the reader know better Michael McColgan, the instrument whom Our Lord and Our Lady have desired to use. It is with hope that those who read this will not misconstrue this reason. The focus of the book is not on Michael but on the messages that have been given to us from Heaven.

Michael McColgan was born in New Jersey on July 26, 1970. He lives with his mother and father and his younger brother. Michael has led the normal life of anyone his age: i.e. competing in sports, going out with friends, and getting involved with academic and social activities. Michael graduated from high school in 1988 and went on to attend college, graduating in May of 1992 and is now a seminarian answering the call of God to the priesthood.

On the eve of his second year in college, after having gone to Medjugorje[1], Michael began receiving messages from the Blessed Mother and her Son, Jesus Christ. Michael, being a normal 19 year old at the time, did not know what to think of the occurrence. It was during prayer in his room, after midnight, on August 17, 1989, that Our Lady spoke to him interiorly for the first time. Our Lady came saying, "I am the Mother of all Mankind." (see message of August 17, 1989). Michael felt an *overwhelming* presence and a peace before, during and after the event. He knew instinctively not to speak of what had happened. It was from this day that Our Lord and Our Lady began to give Michael messages for all the world. In February of 1990, Our Lady told Michael that she would lead him to the priest who was to be his spiritual director. This occurred two months later, as Our Lady had foretold. It was to Father James Sauchelli that Michael confided about the locutions. The messages along with various inner visions have continued to this day and are still being received as this book goes to print.

The guidance of the Blessed Mother and her Son, Jesus, through the messages have led Michael and those around him into a more profound deepening of prayer and a greater desire to receive the sacraments and support the Pope and the Church's Magisterium and teaching, through word and action. Through these messages Our Lord and Our Lady ask us to "open our hearts" and each day grow in a closer union with them.

[1] It is believed that the Blessed Mother has been appearing in Medjugorje (in former Yugoslavia) since June 24, 1981. The apparitions continue to occur every day through the present time.

SUMMARY OF THE MESSAGES
AND THE THREEFOLD CALL OF CHRIST

Simply stated, the messages and visions given to Michael through what the Church's great mystics, St. John of the Cross and St. Teresa of Avila call **intellectual locutions*** and **imaginative visions***, are a call to place Christ at the center of our lives. Mary calls us to follow her Son and thus live the Gospel to the fullest extent of our ability. Indeed, in any time, Christ is the answer, for He is "the Way, the Truth and the Life." (John 14:6) There is woven within the messages an incredibly important threefold call - three points that are consistently expressed by Christ and His Mother. These three points have played a very in-depth role in Michael's life and are at the heart of his call from Christ and an important point of prayer for all of us. They are:

1) **The Holy Eucharist** - Our Lord has given to us this su-preme gift of His love so that He would be with us in an ex-traordinary way until the end of the world. He desires so much for us to adore and love Him and to gain strength from the Eucharist so that we may be able to follow Him each day of our lives. This "call" for us to place our hearts in focus upon the Blessed Sacrament is by far THE central call of the mes-sages — that is, for us to love and participate in the Holy Mass and so to adore and love Jesus, **truly** present in the Most Blessed Sacrament.

2) **Youth and Children** (especially the sick and suffering) - This second call began to unfold on May 3, 1994. It was on May 3, 1994 that Michael received an interior call of such great power that he said it has changed his life forever. This call from Our Lord was in a **very specific** way given to him. This call is for Michael to act as an intercessor — in a very serious way in God's plan — for all children and youth of the world who are sick and suffering. Michael knew immediately with

---

* An explanation of intellectual locutions and imaginative visions can be found in the chapter titled "Locutions and Visions" in the book *Fire Within*, written by Thomas Dubay, S.M., Ignatius Press, San Francisco, 1989.

an unusual clarity that this pertained to all sicknesses and injuries and all sufferings especially those stemming from emotional, physical and sexual abuse. This interior call was followed by messages clarifying this (in words from Our Lady). Michael has repeatedly received confirmations of this special call given to him from Our Lord.

3) **The Church and the Pope** - This call — one and the same — was also given to Michael in a special way (but not in the magnitude of the second point: Youth and Children). Our Lord, simply, has asked Michael and all of us to pray very much for the Holy Father and for the Church and all of its members. This was explained to Michael (and all of us) through various messages culminating on February 15, 1993 when Michael received the "Chaplet of Truth" from the Blessed Mother. The chaplet is spreading and many have begun to pray for the Pope and all priests and religious and the Church in its entirety — Militant, Suffering and Triumphant. Our Lady has asked us to pray the chaplet especially on Thursdays because this was the day that Christ instituted the Holy Eucharist and the Priesthood.

The messages, then, speak concerning many topics but in a special way they call us to love the Blessed Sacrament and thank Jesus for this incredible gift which Pope John Paul II calls "the Sacrament of Love" (from his first encyclical letter, *Redemptor Hominis*) We should bear in mind also that the Holy Father (John Paul II) began perpetual adoration of the Blessed Sacrament in a chapel at St. Peter's on December 2, 1981. This is a powerful example for us to follow. Why would he do this? It is simple: to show us, by his own actions, that we should love and adore Jesus in the Blessed Sacrament. The Eucharist should be central in our lives.

The central core of the messages has now ended, as of February 11, 1995 — Feast of Our Lady of Lourdes. There have been other "gifts" given to Michael so that he may continue to grow in the **fullness** of his calling to follow Our Lord. He has been called, at times, to suffer for souls as a "soul of reparation" or what is commonly known as a "victim soul." Michael has also been given a "gift" of reading souls, which means that he is able to see the state of a soul at times — he is given to understand the soul's trials and sins. Our Lord sometimes gives these "gifts" to souls so that they can be even more powerful instruments in His hands. These gifts began to be unveiled to Michael in the early stage of the messages and have continued to intensify greatly with time, becoming even more specific in May of 1994 with his call to be a close friend of and intercessor for the youth and children of the world who are sick and suffering. As time has gone on, these gifts have occurred more and more and Michael says that they are now a constant experience, especially regarding the ability to read souls, so that Michael can pray for them or help them by speaking with them and thus opening the door of their hearts for Christ to come into their lives and heal them.

All of the above has been explained to you, the reader, so that the **entire** work that Our Lord has wished to do with and through Michael and with all of us (through our prayer) can be realized in its fullness — **all for Christ's glory and honor**. Michael asks that you pray for him and remember that he is **not** the focus of what Our Lord has done and is continuing to do through him. He is *only* an instrument in the hands of Our Lord. Michael said, "May all eyes look toward Mary and her Son, our Savior, Jesus Christ. May all hearts come before Jesus in the Blessed Sacrament. He should be our love and our all."

SHE IS WITH US

Since the time of the end of the central core of the messages to the world through Michael, Our Lady has come to him six times. On April 15, 1995 (Holy Saturday), May 13, 1995 (Feast of Our Lady of the Blessed Sacrament), September 19 and 22, 1995, November 2, 1995 and December 7, 1995. Our Lord has come to Michael four times. On August 15, 1995 (Feast of the Assumption), November 7 and 14, 1995 and December 7, 1995.

There was also one vision that Michael received, to further confirm his calling by Our Lord concerning the children and youth of the world. It occurred at the end of August 1995, while Michael was in prayer before the Blessed Sacrament (in the Adoration Chapel in his home Church). He explains: "I was kneeling before the Blessed Sacrament; exposed in the Monstrance, when the walls of the room suddenly were not there. Behind me and on each side of me there were *multitudes* of children and youth. We were all in silent prayer before Our Lord, truly present in the Blessed Sacrament. I *knew* and *understood* fully during this time that I was in a special and particular way interceding on their behalf and my heart was overcome with a great emotion and love for *all* of them. I knew that with me were children and youth, sick and suffering in many different ways, from all over the world; from every country and walk of life."

The messages of April 15, May 13, August 15, September 22, November 7 and 14, and December 7 are included for the benefit of the reader. The messages of September 19 and November 2 are not because of their particular nature. Of them Michael says, "It is very important that we realize the great gift that God has given to us in allowing our Mother to come to us. May we all realize what this means: that she is with us. So let us, then, "open our hearts" with great love for her and her Son, Our Lord and Savior, Jesus Christ."

"I AM THERE ... FOR ALL"

On November 7, 1995, Our Lord once again called Michael to come before Him, where He is truly present, in the Tabernacle. Michael states, "I was overwhelmingly drawn to Him; to love Him; to adore Him." A short time into being before the Tabernacle, Our Lord spoke to Michael, asking him, "Will you stay with Me and ease the pains of My heart caused by the ingratitude of so many?"

Michael said that at these words he was overcome with love for our Lord. Love *consumed* him in those moments and for a time after. Michael wished to share this experience because he says that we are *all* called by Our Lord to come to Him and spend time with Him; before His Real Presence in the Holy Eucharist. Jesus wishes for all of us to come to Him so that we may love Him and He may love us in return.

On November 14, 1995, while Michael was in prayer contemplating the Holy Eucharist – Michael said, "Our Lord spoke to me with great seriousness and power, engraving His words upon my heart." Our Lord said:

"I AM THERE ... FOR ALL"

Our Lord was referring to His *true* presence in the Most Blessed Sacrament when He said, "I am there ..." and then "for all," meaning for all people.

May we love and adore Jesus, Our Lord and Savior, in the Most Blessed Sacrament of the Altar. Let us thank Him everyday for this most wonderful gift.

LET US BE OPEN TO THE CALL

Our Lady has been with us for some time. Our Lady continues to call us with a great love because she wishes us to open our hearts to her so that she can lead us to Jesus. Our Lady comes for this reason; to make Jesus the center of our lives so that we will have peace. To have this peace we need to open our hearts in a sincere way. To be "open" to living the messages means to want to live them with our hearts, not just with our minds. It means to pray and read Scripture every day, because in doing so, we strengthen our relationship with Jesus and Mary. Our Lady invites us, also, to pray the Rosary and to meditate on its mysteries, to understand, in a greater way, the lives of Jesus and Mary.

In our prayer we come closer to Jesus and Mary because we understand their suffering and in that understanding we gain knowledge of how to carry our crosses and how to live our lives. Prayer, Our Lady tells us, is our greatest weapon. Why does she say this? Because it is in prayer that we come closer to Jesus. It is our dialogue with God. When we strengthen our relationship with God, then we, in a sense, have more armor to protect ourselves from sin and the devil's temptations. By our prayer, we call Our Lord and His Mother to be with us, to help us, to protect us, to guide us onto the path of virtue. It is through prayer that we gain peace. Let us open our hearts. Let us pray because we desire to be closer with Jesus and Mary, because we desire to be closer to God, the Father. Let us always be open to the inspiration of the Holy Spirit in our lives.

Let us live conversion. This "conversion" means to decide for God. Our Lady calls us to conversion in our lives. This means to weed out all those things which take us away from getting to know Jesus better. We need to turn away from anything that is an obstacle for us to be able to live the Gospel message. For this end, Our Lady says, "Pray, fast, do penance (go to Confession and be aware of sin) be at peace (live love and forgiveness in our lives) and live conversion (decide for God in all things and at all times)." **Our Lady's message is one of Hope.** Let us focus on this hope as we try to live the Gospel message every day of our lives.

I would ask everyone to look seriously at the messages; to read them over and over again so that you (and I) may gain a deeper understanding of Our Lady's call. Our Lady's message is one of urgency and great seriousness, but it is more so one of love, of peace, and of hope. Our

Mother is with us. Let us be open to her call, so that we may grow in our love for the Holy Mass and for Jesus, who is truly present in the Holy Eucharist. Let us be open to the Holy Spirit in prayer every day. Let us love and forgive one another. In essence, let us love Jesus above all the things of this world, which will pass away, and let us allow Jesus to fill our hearts with His peace. Let us open the doors of our hearts ... He is patiently knocking ... if we turn off the calls of the world we will hear Our Lord's voice ... "I am the Way, the Truth, and the Life..." (John 14:6)

I would ask all of you who read this to make a Holy Hour before our Lord, once a week. This is a great means of reparation and of showing Jesus that you love Him. During your Holy Hour, please pray, especially for the love and respect of human life in all of its stages with all of its joys and sorrows. Take time out of your week and make an "Hour of Life." Please, think about doing this.

The Eucharist should be the center of our lives. I would like to share a few words with you spoken by our Holy Father, John Paul II, on the importance of Holy Mass and the Eucharist in his life. Following his example, may all of us continually grow in our love for Mass and the Eucharist

> "The priest is a man of the Eucharist. In the span of nearly 50 years of priesthood, what is still the most important and most sacred moment for me is the celebration of the Eucharist. My awareness of celebrating *in persona Christi* at the altar prevails. Never in the course of these years have I failed to celebrate the Most Holy Sacrifice. If this has occurred, it has been due entirely to reasons independent of my will. **Holy Mass is the absolute center of my life and of everyday of my life.**"

> John Paul II
> given on October 27, 1995 to Cardinals, Bishops
> and priests. (Excerpted from *L'Observatore
> Romano*, N.46, Nov. 15, 1995 weekly edition, pg 7;
> *Priests Need to be Men of Prayer*)

May God bless and protect all of us and may Our Lady wrap us in her mantle of love.

— Michael McColgan

DEDICATION

This book is dedicated to Our Lady, Mother of All Mankind, and Her Son, Our Lord and Savior, Jesus Christ. It is He that she wishes us to know and love through these messages. Let us open our hearts and respond with love and with sincerity to her call.

Thank you to Bernadette, Bonnie, Ray, Walt, and all those who helped make this publication possible. May all hearts be open.

IT SHALL COME TO PASS . . .

It shall come to pass in the last days, says God, that I will pour out a portion of My spirit upon all mankind: Your sons and daughters shall dream dreams. Indeed, upon My servants and My handmaids I will pour out a portion of My Spirit in those days, and they shall prophesy. And I will work wonders in the heavens above, and signs on the earth below: blood, fire, and a cloud of smoke. The sun shall be turned to darkness, and the moon to blood, before the coming of that great and glorious day of the Lord. Then shall everyone be saved who calls on the name of the Lord.

Acts 2: 17-21

What Does Our Lady Ask Us To Do?

Attend Mass

To grow in the desire to participate in the Holy Sacrifice of the Mass and to receive Jesus, truly present in the Eucharist.

Eucharistic Adoration

To come before Jesus, in the Blessed Sacrament, realizing His TRUE presence before us. Making a Holy Hour, specifically making an "Hour for Life;" praying and making reparation for all sins against life: (ie:abortion, artificial birth control, fetal testing and experimentation and euthanasia.) And asking Jesus to pour forth His mercy upon the world.

Prayer

Making time in our day to speak with God from our hearts - to strengthen our relationship with Him; praying the Holy Rosary and the Divine Mercy Chaplet. Reading and meditating on Sacred Scripture.

Monthly Confession

Making each Confession a true conversion of the heart with a sincere and firm purpose of amendment.

Fasting

Our Lady asks us to fast on bread and water, but we can also fast on other things — like giving up smoking cigarettes, watching TV, or listening to music for a day.

Reconciliation

Our Lady calls us to reconcile ourselves with God and with those around us. She asks us to be forgiving with our family members, friends, and with those at work and school. It is important, she says, to work on making peace within our relationships.

* The reader should know that the messages are meant for everyone. Many times Our Lord and Our Lady, in speaking to Michael, say, "my child." When you are reading the messages, though, read them with the understanding that Our Lord and Our Lady are speaking, as well, to you individually. The messages are meant for each one of us.

OPEN YOUR HEARTS

*Messages from Our Lord Jesus and His Blessed Mother,
given to Michael McColgan through inner locution
from August 17, 1989 through the present time.*

DEFINITION OF INNER LOCUTION

This is a supernatural means of communication. It is not a sensory communication since none of the five bodily senses are involved. They are messages given in very clear words, words which are not formed in the mind of the person, but in the heart, while the mind of the person is at rest. It is different from an exterior locution in which the person hears an audible voice through the ear.

All messages are from the Blessed Mother except where indicated.

MESSAGES FROM THE YEAR 1989

AUGUST 17, 1989 — I am the Mother of all Mankind. Through me the world will find peace, for through me all will know my Son, Jesus. I am the Queen of Peace. I wish you all to pray to ease my heart and so to ease your suffering.

AUGUST 21, 1989 — My children, hold the Rosary close to you and I will be there to give you peace. My children, I am with you always.

NOVEMBER 27, 1989 — My child, please stay close to my Immaculate Heart and the path of my Son, Jesus. Do not look to the world any more. See how I am leading you away from its snares, from Satan's temptations. See how I am leading you on a holy path, a path I wish you to follow. My Son is heavily burdened with the sins of the world and God's justice is soon to come. The world does not know what awaits it for its sins.

Please, turn only to me. Let me enfold you in my mantle. Be simple, humble, and full of love. I have given you the wisdom to realize much. Thank God for what He has done for you through me. Thank Jesus for His never-ending mercy. Use this wisdom to turn from sin. My Son and I are with you always. Please, pray more. Make your day a continuous prayer. In prayer I can make you stronger and better guide you to holiness. My light surrounds you always.

DECEMBER 1, 1989 — My child, pray continuously. Follow every word that I have told you. Live the messages, which I have given the world. Do all that I have asked and follow the path, which God has made for you. Know that I am with you always and that I love you with a Mother's heart. Pray, pray continuously, and you will be able to accomplish everything.

OPEN YOUR HEARTS

MESSAGES FROM THE YEAR 1990

FEBRUARY 1, 1990 — My child ... purity and innocence. Let me guide you. Open your heart completely to me. Do not hold back. Let me fill you with my Immaculate presence. Let me enshroud you with my light. Follow the path of humility always and hold dear to your purity and innocence. I love you.

FEBRUARY 2, 1990 (JESUS) — My child, please pray more. Pray for those who DO trespass against the wishes of My Father, and who trample on My Sacred Heart, forcing the thorns surrounding it to deepen and so cause Me greater pain. My child, please come and visit Me. I am all alone. Come in adoration before the Blessed Sacrament. By your prayers make amends. Continue to reinforce and spread My wish for more adoration of the Blessed Sacrament. Tell My children to come and ask for forgiveness. My mercy is never-ending for all souls. My graces shall pour forth upon them in great abundance.

    * It is important to note that in the first and second messages from Our Lord to Michael that Jesus draws us to come to Him in the Blessed Sacrament, where He is truly present in the tabernacles of our churches. He also asks us to pray and to make reparation for sin, which causes His Most Sacred Heart so much pain.

FEBRUARY 2, 1990 — My child, listen to my Son. Please follow His wishes and know that I am with you through all of your trials. I love you.

FEBRUARY 9, 1990 (JESUS) — My dear child, please listen to Me. Come to Me in silence. Come and visit Me in the tabernacle where I am so ignored and so alone. Come and visit Me. Take time and pray for forgiveness for those in the world who turn away and ignore My great gift to them. Come to Me so that I may make of you a great light, so that many will see Me. You will help lead them to Me. I love you. Please, come and visit with Me.

FEBRUARY 11, 1990 (JESUS) — My child, the light of My Mother is now entering the world so powerfully and so strongly. My great enemy, the lurid and dark Satan, knows that his time is almost gone. He feels it already slipping from his hands. You see this light, with which My Father is flooding the earth. Follow this light. Always stay in this light. Do not lose sight of it. Listen only to My Mother's beating heart. It, like her voice, is so soft, so tender, but enfolds all the power, which will crush in finality the head of My enemy, the Serpent.

Look at all the changes in the world. They are not mankind's doing. All of this has happened because of those who have listened to Me, because of those who are continuing to let their hearts and lives be lit in this great light of Mine, which My Mother is, by her appearances, spreading on the earth. Heaven is rejoicing, for the time has come. The angels are crying out in joy because My word and the wishes of My Eternal Father will soon cover the earth and peace will come.

My child, My Mother gazes upon you with such sweet tenderness. Consecrate some time each day to easing the pain of her Immaculate Heart, caused by the non-believers, by speaking with her from your heart, by praying with her from your heart, and by doing all that she asks of you during every moment of your day. Continue also to bring yourself closer to Me. Continue to venerate My Sacred Heart, covered in thorns by those who ignore My Mother and by those who do not respect or acknowledge her, therein not respecting My wishes or those of My Father.

The time is coming very soon when all of mankind will see the justice for its great sin, for its refusal of Me, for its refusal of My Mother, for its refusal of the Father in Heaven, and for its refusal of those who listened to Me and who did what I asked of them. Tell all those who believe that they must pray more, that Holy Mass should become more important to them and that if they listen to My Mother and follow her and do all that she wishes I will increase their graces one-hundred fold.

Let silence speak to you, My child. Do not watch television. Do not listen to so much music. Pray more! Visit Me more in your heart. Keep Me with you always. Open yourself and let Me use you as a tool. Let yourself become an instrument of Mine. Hold My Mother close to your heart. She will give you strength through humility. She will lead you to Me. She will let you know all that you need to do. Please, tell all of My children to pray. Pray especially the Rosary, for it eases the pain of My Mother's heart so, and so much does it soothe the burning from the sword that constantly pierces her heart. Look at her tears, tears of blood ... that is how much she longs for humanity to listen to her and return back to God. That is how much she loves her children, who are all of the peoples of the earth.

Gaze upon My Mother's heart and you will also see the sorrow in My heart. Pray, My child. Pray and be silent. Stand strong, for Satan will try and seduce your thoughts. Immerse yourself in My Mother and Me and he will not be able to harm you. Know that I love you, always. You are My child, forever.

FEBRUARY 23, 1990 — My child, I am coming to all the world now with my arms outstretched. I welcome everyone to come with their hearts open and ready to receive God. I love my children so much. I am calling them with all my heart. I am now imploring you all. The time is very near for the events of which I have been speaking to you. Humanity must decide for God. If not, very serious calamities will fall upon it.

My Son is calling all of the world back to the ways of God. He is doing this act of mercy through me, the Woman Clothed in the Sun, His Mother of the Sorrowful Heart. Please, open yourselves to me. Open your hearts to the great mercy which my Son is pouring upon humanity, flooding the world in a great light. Please, come to me, my dear children, convert yourselves, decide for God in everything you do. Let God fill your lives with His great love and His peace.

Time is falling short for all. I plead with you to look upon your Mother, to look upon the tears that fall from my face in such great sorrow for you. Listen to my voice that descends over you asking you to turn your eyes to my Son, who suffers still because of humanity's indifference to my call. His blood, which now is shed in mercy for all, will soon purify the earth and cover it in God's peace, which my Son brought with Him when He came the first time and which He is bringing through the victory of my Immaculate Heart.

Please, my child, pray for all the unbelievers in the world and for all of the youth and families in the world. Many of the young people today are being viciously attacked by Satan. Please, pray specifically for them. Hold time with me for this intention. Thank you for having responded to my wishes. Continue to open your heart to my Son and to me. I love you and I am continually watching over you.

FEBRUARY 26, 1990 — My child, please continue to follow along the path, which I have with my Son, made for you. Let nothing get in your way of doing my work. I am with you always. When every temptation and difficulty presents itself, I am there with you holding your hand. Like a little child you tremble and my motherly touch and embrace enfolds you and wishes to warm your heart. I want all of my children to know that I am close to them, that I am their Mother, now and always. You must also spread the message of my Son. Time is growing short for all of mankind. Humanity does not know what is coming because people continue to ignore my Son's calling through me. People are drowning out my loving plea with the proud and aggressive voice of the world, the voice of my adversary, Satan. That voice has grown so loud because many on earth join in and shout with him.

The hour is soon to come upon all of you though, when the humble and loving voice of your Mother shall cover and drown that of the adversary and all those who follow him. Please, my child, you must come to me more in your day. Please, pray more! I need your prayers. I need and want you to follow in the desires and wishes of your Blessed Mother, who is soon to be victorious with her Son over all the darkness, which has covered such a great part of the earth.

Please, listen to my voice and follow my call at all times in your day and know that I am always with you.

FEBRUARY 28, 1990 — My child, I have increased my appearances all over the world because time grows shorter for all of humanity, which at this time is not in a great way listening to its Mother. Only a few of my children listen to me and choose to live the messages. I speak to you as a gentle and loving Mother so that in confusion my voice becomes a rock for you to lean on and cling to.

I am with you always, ... watching over you and protecting you in everything you do. I love you, my child.

MARCH 9, 1990 — My children, come back to my Son. My arms are open for you and tears fall from my eyes. Please, listen to my call. Please, respond with your whole heart. You can do this only through prayer and fasting. Pray and fast. Come to me and comfort my heart, which is pierced by the sharp sword of humanity's sins. Come in silence and prayer. I will fill you with such a thirst for the peace of Heaven.

OPEN YOUR HEARTS

Open your heart so that my Son and I may enter and like the coming spring make of you a new and fresh bud for the world to see. Be humble always. Pray, pray, pray, ... pray please, my child. I love you.

MARCH 11, 1990 — Dear children, look to the Father in Heaven, Who, in great mercy, has sent me down to earth and with my arms outstretched over all of humanity, I am pouring upon all of you God's love and His peace. Listen to what I tell you, for the messages are the words of my Son, Who is now both pleading and calling mankind. Thank you my children ...

MARCH 12, 1990 — My dear child, ... come to me in silence. Turn off the world and pray. Come and comfort my heart, which is so upset and sorrowful over humanity's answer to my Son. Come and visit my Son, who is all alone in the tabernacle hour after hour. He waits patiently. He waits patiently for all to come and see Him, not with their eyes, but with their hearts. Pray every day. Pray with your heart. Open your heart to my Son so that He may plant His seed in you and make of you a bright light in the darkness. Listen to all that you hear Him say to you. Spread the word and live my messages, therein becoming a living example to those around you.

Love everyone. Make love the center of your life. Make Jesus the center of your life. Love and Jesus are the same. Know that the mercy shall become greater. God is now opening the "Flood gates" so to say, upon humanity. Pray, my child, that the world does not turn away from Him. Pray! Close your eyes and bring your heart to me. Open your heart when you pray. Say after all of your prayers:

Mary, Mother of the Sorrowful Heart, may our prayers ease the pains caused by the great sins of the world. May we follow your lead and live the messages, which you give to the world. May our hearts be open to God always and may we live in the love and peace of Jesus Christ. Amen.

My Son and I are always with you. Turn off the world and listen to the constant voice of God. I love you ...

MARCH 12, 1990 (JESUS) - SECOND MESSAGE — My child, as you sit here in the silence, do you not understand what I am asking of you, so that you may feel this peace always? Let the breeze blow around you. It is gentle like My love for you ... for all of My children.

Today is a beautiful day. It is the first real day of spring to come to where you are. Look around and see all the smiles, all the joy in the warmth of the day. See how friendship is flowing. This is why My love for you is likened to that of spring. Because when it enters your heart you blossom as a flower does when it receives the water and the sun. The earth that the flower is in, is God the Father, as He is everything. The water is the refreshing Holy Spirit, which floods the hearts of those who open themselves to Me. The sun is Myself, the light which leads you through the darkness, the warmth which enters your heart and fills you with the burning desire for Me and for all that I wish for you. Listen to Me always, My child, and stay by My Mother, as she will lead you to the truth and the light and happiness, which await all of you in Heaven. Be silent in your heart and you will be radiant to the world.

MARCH 13, 1990 (JESUS) — My child, the voice of My Mother is also My voice, for she has done all that the Father has asked, ... humbly and obediently. I, too, ask of all of My children the same ... to come to Me with hearts open, ... ready to do as I ask of them, ready to love everyone that they meet and see Me in everyone around them. Today, again, My Father has blessed you with a beautiful day, physically and spiritually. As the wind surrounds and caresses you so does My love, My mercy, and My peace.

The sun can shine every day in your hearts, only if you let it be so, ... only if you ask Me to come and enter and there I can show you what graces I have waiting for you. I will replace your heart with Mine. I will show you the true and divine love of the Holy Trinity. Open yourselves by praying. Open yourselves by taking time out of your day to talk with Me from your heart. Let Me explain it to you. I, your loving Jesus, am like a good friend. The more you wish to see Me, the more you wish to spend time with Me, the closer we become; the more we are bonded in love ... just as it is with your friends on Earth. This is why I say that each one of you should see Me in the other. I am present in each one of you. The more you open yourselves to each other, the more you understand and care for each other. You do the same when you pray or when you take time in your day to speak with Me from your heart.

I, like a good friend, can then be with you and can truly show My love to you, for you have wanted it to be so; and so the more you will comprehend My undying love for you.

I love you now and always. I leave it up to you as I have given each of you the free will to choose. What greatly upsets Me is that you do not choose Me, but the things of this world, which can not give you true peace. Only I, your God, can give you true peace in your life. I love you, and as I always have, I wish to be your best friend. Come and talk with Me. Share your feelings with Me. Open yourselves up to Me so that you and I can be intimate; so that I may unite Myself with you as I do in the Eucharist. I love you. Listen to My Mother. Live the messages she brings. Live with, and in, the love of God. Love everyone. Continue to pray and make reparation for the sins committed against My Immaculate Mother. Through your prayers ease the great sufferings of her heart.

The sword, which pierces her Immaculate Heart, sinks deeper each day, causing My Mother more pain. Why? Because of the world's great sin. Love always and thank the Father in Heaven for the great gifts He bestows upon all of mankind. My mercy will flood the earth more in the future. None of the world can fully imagine or understand this great hour.

Begin by opening your hearts to My Father and Myself. The heart was made to hold all that I can give to you, but you must want it. My graces are ready to come upon you. Pray, pray, pray at all times. Unite yourself with Me in prayer so that I may further lead you ... let Me take you by the hand My child. Live in My love.

MARCH 13, 1990 - SECOND MESSAGE — My child, continue to immerse yourself in prayer while meditating on the great sorrow which my Immaculate Heart suffers. Come to me more often during your day. Come to me every day. Pray with a greater intensity each time; thus, through your words, ease the pain which is caused by the sword of humanity's sin and ignorance of its loving and Eternal God. I grow so distressed because you do not truly listen to what I ask of you. Still I look upon you with loving eyes. My love for you is so very great. If one drop of the love of my heart for you would touch yours you, would not be able to stop your tears because of the great joy that would overcome you.

Know that I love every one of my children and that my arms are outstretched and waiting for you to come to me, your Mother. Come my children, so beloved of my Son, Jesus, and of me. My child, begin to turn away from the world and its voice more and more. Listen only to the gentle voice of my Son and myself. Pray continuously and then I will be able to fulfill all of my plans for you. I love you.

MARCH 15, 1990 (JESUS) — My child, I am asking you to listen seriously and to live what I tell you because I wish others to learn by your actions. Also, by living My words, you will better be able to help people understand My love for them, especially when you speak with them. They will see it all over you, almost as a glow. Please, My child, close your eyes and open your heart. For then you will truly be able to see better than if you only used your eyes. Open the eyes of your heart. Do this through prayer, especially, through the prayer of the Rosary. This prayer ... so beloved of My Mother. When the words leave your lips, they surround and caress her heart. This prayer from your heart is like a song to My Mother, who loves you so much.

Remind and tell everyone of the Rosary's great importance. The wonders you see all over the world at this time are occurring because My people are finally listening to My call. My love and My peace are being born now in so many of My children, thus creating a domino-like effect. Soon, all the world will be covered in My love and My mercy, like a fire.

My justice will also come as a fire. Only you can decide and choose, because of the free will I have given you, which fire will come upon you. I love so very much. This is why I have sent My Mother to you, to help you understand My great love for you, ... so that you will choose the fire of My love and not the fire of My imminent justice. Know that I love you all and that I am waiting for you at all times. Please, come to Me now. Soon it will be too late, My child. Let My people know this. Tell them that I wish them to decide now. I love you. Live in My love and My peace, which I send upon you all.

MARCH 17, 1990 (JESUS) — My child, live My messages. Love everyone. Love in everything you do and then you will see Me in everyone and everything. Then you will know My peace. Pray, also, in everything. My Mother wishes of you humility and simplicity. Go in My peace.

MARCH 21, 1990 (JESUS) — My child, listen to the sighs of My Mother. Look at the tears which fall from her eyes. Contemplate her great sorrow over man's decision to turn away from God ... upon her children's decision to turn away from the caring of their Mother. Let everyone know that My Mother knows a "mother's pain." Tell My people that My Mother understands why they are so sad and this is why she wishes them, all mothers, to turn to her. She will give them comfort. She will help them understand and accept their crosses, with love. For I love all of My children and will not abandon them.

This evening at Mass you, My child, saw the sadness on the faces of so many of My children. They have let themselves be caught up by the "adult" world. Their faith in Me has drowned and is drowning, in a sea of confusion ... the world's confusion. They are trapped in the ways which My adversary has set. They have lost their way. They no longer know their Father because they have not been with Him for so long. Pray for them. Pray that they may hear My call and that when they do, for they will, ... they will respond and live as I wish them to, in love and in peace.

Today's scripture reading was about My meeting with the Samaritan woman at the well. The words I spoke to her then carry as much weight now ... "If you drink of this water you shall be thirsty again, but the water I shall give you, the one of life, will replenish you for eternity." All My children need is Me. I am awaiting their return with open arms, ... as I have sent My Mother to call each of them by name. Pray, My child. Pray and be silent. I love you. Go in the peace which I give you.

MARCH 21, 1990 - SECOND MESSAGE — My child, you are so beloved to me. I need you to continue to follow along the path, which I, with my Son, have made for you. Continue on this road with prayer, simplicity, and humility. I am with you at every step along this path. I have accounted for everything, so do not fear. I have taken hold of your hand, and as I am your Mother, I will lead you. I am with you always.

MARCH 21, 1990 (JESUS) - THIRD MESSAGE — My child, so beloved of My Mother. I wish you to close off your mind and ears from the call of the world. Do not pay any attention to the calls of sin. Close your eyes and immerse yourself into My love for you — into My Mother's love for you. I ask you to love. Open your heart and love. Know that I love you and that I will protect you. Your Guardian Angel is with you at every moment, as I am with you, also, at every moment. Close your eyes to the world and open them for what I have prepared for you, the purification of your soul and the pure love which I want to pour into your heart.

Open yourself to Me. Tell everyone that I need them to open themselves to Me. I need them to be ready to accept what I give to them. Open yourselves. Open the eyes of your soul and see the light, the great light, of My mercy and love. I love you always.

MARCH 21, 1990 (JESUS) - FOURTH MESSAGE — My child, tell My people that I wish for them to come and visit Me. Tell them that during Adoration of the Blessed Sacrament many, many graces are received. Tell My children that I love them so very much and that I am awaiting their return to Me. I am here for you at every moment.

MARCH 22, 1990 — My child, please follow my messages. Please, live them with your heart. Only then can I work in you. Fasting and prayer are so very important in warding off Satan's attacks. Please pray and ward off my adversary with the special prayer of the Rosary. Pray the Rosary. Let me work in you. For me to be able to do this you must pray and fast. I do not wish to admonish you, but only teach you to love. My son and I are always with you.

MARCH 23, 1990 — My child, please listen to me. I need you to fast more and to pray more. Tonight you recalled how this year you have been tempted so much by the devil. This will continue. You can help destroy him, though, and help my plans succeed in the face of ever increasing danger in the world. I say danger, because if the world does not begin to listen to me, then it is in very serious danger.

Come back to God. Return to Him with your hearts open. Open yourselves to the gift He wishes to give you. Please, listen now! Tell my children that they must listen to me and that they should not wait but believe now. Pray for the unbelievers. Pray, also, for all the youth of the world and all families. Pray, pray, pray!

I love you, as a Mother does, and I am keeping watch over you, my child, ... over all of My children.

(The Locutionist then prayed 3 Glory Be's, then Mary began to speak to him again.)

Continue to write ... I shed tears of blood. Why? Because the world has no idea what will become of it if it does not return to God. The world will burn and the fire will consume almost every part of the earth. If the world does not listen, this will come. I do not want this, my children. This is why I cry tears of blood.

Please, pray this prayer in union with my great sorrow, ... open your hearts ...

Oh, Mary, Mother of Sorrows, please intercede for us before your Son, Jesus Christ, we beg you. Mother of the Most Immaculate and Sorrowful Heart, be our refuge in this time of great danger. Watch over us at all times, we pray;

Mother of All Mankind, we love you
Mother of Our Lord, Jesus Christ, Our Savior, we love you
Mother of such great sorrow, we love you
Mother Mary, Daughter of God the Father,
Whitest Lily in the Garden of Heaven, we, your children, love you.

We come to you with open hearts, please guide us to your Son, Jesus Christ, and may you, Mary, our Blessed Mother, be with us always. Amen

I love you all, my dear children, and I send you the peace of my Son, Jesus. Go in God's Peace.

* In this message Our Lady says, "... the fire will consume almost every part of the earth." In Fatima, Portugal, in 1917, in an apparition, Our Lady said in one message, "Various nations will be annihilated."

13

In Akita, Japan, Our Lady came from 1973 to 1981 to a nun named Sr. Agnes Sasagawa. The revelations from the Blessed Mother and from Sr. Agnes' Guardian Angel have received the full approval of the Church.

On October 13, 1973, Our Lady gave a very serious message to Sr. Agnes ... a message that, in part, is like the one revealed to Michael on March 23, 1990. Sr. Agnes writes in her journal: "Taking up my Rosary I knelt down and made the Sign of the Cross. Hardly had I finished when that Voice of indescribable beauty came from the statue to my deaf ears. From the first word I prostrated myself to the ground concentrating all my attention:

'My dear daughter, listen well to what I have to say to you. You will inform your superior.' And then after a short silence: 'As I told you, if men do not repent and better themselves, the Father will inflict a terrible punishment on all humanity. It will be a punishment greater than the deluge, such as has never have been before. Fire will fall down from the sky and will wipe out a great part of humanity ... the good as well as the bad, sparing neither priests nor faithful. The survivors will find themselves so desolate that they will envy the dead. The only arms which will remain for you will be the Rosary and the Sign left by my Son. Each day recite the prayers of the Rosary. With the Rosary pray for the Pope, the bishops, and the priests. The work of the devil will infiltrate even into the Church in such a way that one will see cardinals opposing cardinals, bishops against other bishops. The priests who venerate me will be scorned and opposed by their confreres, churches and altars sacked, the Church will be full of those who accept compromises and the demon will press many priests and consecrated souls to leave the service of the Lord. The demon will be especially implacable against souls consecrated to God. The thought of the loss of so many souls is the cause of my sadness. If sins increase in number and gravity, there will no longer be pardon for them. With courage speak to your superior. He will know how to encourage each one of you to pray and to accomplish works of reparation.'

"When the voice was quiet, I gathered the courage to raise my head and I saw the statue still brilliant in light, but a slight expression of sadness seemed to veil her face. Our Lady spoke again ... 'Pray very much the prayers of the Rosary. I alone am still able to save you from the calamities which approach. Those who place their confidence in me will be saved.' She had finished speaking."

These messages from Our Lady are indeed very strong, but the reader should remember that God's justice is not the focus of Our Lady's messages. Her message is one of **HOPE.** We should focus on prayer, Confession, and peace in our lives. We should focus on the Holy Mass and on cultivating a greater love for Jesus, truly present in the Blessed Sacrament. Let us not focus on chastisements, but on Jesus.

APRIL 9, 1990 — The time is short before God sends the great chastisement. Pray, my children. Do not become lazy. Do not let Satan pull you away from time that could be put to praying. Please, pray the Rosary every day. I want to thank you for the prayers and reparation that you have offered to God. Please continue ... for many souls are on the road to perdition. Today, also, I ask you to pray especially for young priests. I love you, my children. I love you.

APRIL 9, 1990 - SECOND MESSAGE — My child, do not worry, for I am with you at all times. I love you and I will never abandon you. Pray the Rosary. Tell all my children that I need them to pray the Rosary every day. The Rosary is your greatest weapon! It is the one which levels Satan to the ground and which puts more weight to my heel. The time is short for mankind. The time to return to God is very short. My children, the great battle is now! Take up your crosses. Jesus will help you carry your crosses. Ask Him for help. He will help you. He will sustain you. Pray, my children, for Satan is becoming even more active as I speak with you. Prayer forms a sharper sword for St. Michael and a stronger shield of my presence with you. My children, please listen to your Mother. I love you.

APRIL 9, 1990 - THIRD MESSAGE — Look at the children around you. How innocent and pure they are. See the look of their belief in love. Only the world, with its great darkness covers the eyes of these children. In the beginning all of God's children are pure and innocent. Look at the children and see the face of my Son, Jesus. Jesus lives in the little children. They are amazed even with a butterfly, unlike the prideful men of the world now. Why? Because they have lost the way to love.

They have created their own way to happiness. But this is not the road which God wants them to follow, and this is why they fall to ruin.

They have become even more childish than the little children because they refuse love. To love is to be courageous and noble, under and with God. To love is to have simplicity and humility to accept all that God gives. To love God is to have true peace in the heart. The world must begin to love. Man must begin to love. If you cannot forgive your brother, how can you expect God to forgive you? I do not wish to admonish you, my children, but you must begin to realize that you are in great danger. Look at the heart of the world. It is a dying ember. One by one the fire of each person's heart is dying and so many of my children's hearts are dark and cold. I have come to light the fire in your hearts with the light of Jesus' love and mercy. I have come to help you find the road of God and to lovingly take up your crosses and be purified in the trial of your cross ... the cross which Jesus gives you out of His love. Your cross is not a punishment. It is another step in making the light in your hearts burn brighter. Thus the heart of the world will again burn as bright as the sun. I come to you with the love and mercy of Jesus. LOVE, my children. Love is the key to your happiness. Love and become again, in Jesus, God's little children.

APRIL 10, 1990 — My children, kneel before the Cross in prayer. Pray before my Son, who still feels the pain in His heart because man is so greatly sinful and ignorant of His wishes. The blood now gushes forth from His wounds and also my Sorrowful Heart feels the greater presence of the sword piercing it, because the world is closing itself off to God's mercy. These are the last times. As I have said, the time is very short before what God sends will cover the darkness and hideousness of the earth, thus creating the new light in the purified people to come. The blood of the martyrs and of the aborted babies is crying out for God's justice. This justice is soon to come, my children. Please, respond to the voice and call of your Mother. I wish to lead you out of the sea of iniquity in which humanity is drowning. I wish to lead you to the peace and love of my Son. I wish to lead you to the true joys of life. Please, decide for the way of life to which God is calling each one of you. I am with you always, my dear children, and I, as your Mother, carry and protect you in my heart. Decide for God, my children.

APRIL 10, 1990 - SECOND MESSAGE — My child, I am now over-flowing with tears because of the sins of mankind and because this is the time when I need my children to listen so intently. Now, though, the majority of my children are not listening. Please, tell my darling ones, who are hearing my voice, that I need their prayers so that their broth-ers and sisters may hear God's calling. Then peace will come to the world under the reign of my Son. Pray much for the unbelievers.

APRIL 13, 1990 GOOD FRIDAY — My child, this is my most griev-ous hour. This is when the sword in my heart pierces me with the most pain. Look upon the Cross. Understand the great importance of the Cross. I love you, my children. Please hold the Cross close to your heart at this hour. Pray with me. I love you and want you to know that my Son and I shall never abandon you in your times of distress.

APRIL 15, 1990 EASTER SUNDAY (JESUS) — I am calling all of My children back to Me. With open arms I am asking them to receive Me into their hearts. My mercy is being shed upon all the world. I love each one of you. My death and resurrection was for all of mankind. Return to the Father. Find the true peace which I wish so much to give to you.

APRIL 18, 1990 — My child, I want you to close your eyes and hold tight to your Rosary at this time. I need you to pray. Please, pray espe-cially for the young, who are being deceived and destroyed with the great iniquity that the devil has brought. They, the innocent and pure, are being cut and are bleeding on the thorn bushes sown from the evil seeds of my adversary, Satan. Jesus is calling out to you and with open arms wishes to pour out His great mercy upon you. Know, my chil-dren, that soon His justice will come. I, your Mother, wish to guide you. I will lead you to Jesus so that some of you will see and then be able to lead my other children, who are blind, to salvation.

I am the light of the dawn. My Son's words to mankind now are, 'look to my Mother.' My beloved ones, I am here for you. Please re-nounce sin and pray. I love you and I tell you do not be afraid, for I will protect you with my mantle. Not even Satan himself can harm you then. I love you, my children.

APRIL 19, 1990 (JESUS) — My child, I am coming at a time when the world is in its greatest distress ... covered in a great darkness. I have come to show My people that I am the fullness of life. If they choose the darkness now, then they shall live in the darkness forever. If they choose the light, then they will live in the light forever. I am your loving and merciful Jesus. Please, My children, come to Me. Let Me enter into your hearts where I may be able to show you the love of My Father, where I may give you true peace. My people have not been turning to Me, though. Turn from Satan. My Mother will soon fully crush his head. She is calling all of you before it is too late. Come to Me now, before the great storm begins.

APRIL 27, 1990 — My child, come to me with your eyes closed and your heart open. Come to me in prayer. I wish you to start saying the prayers that I have given to you. I wish you to make them known, but do not relate the source and events as of yet. Come to me in silence with your soul open to the mercy of God. Please, allow me to fill you with the peace of my Son, Jesus. Today, again, you saw the miracle of the sun. This is a gift to you from God. Jesus wishes you to know, through this great sign, that He is always with you and that His mercy is open to flow upon you. I, your Mother, love you so very much. Do not offend God anymore. Be strong, Jesus and I are with you, ... always ...

APRIL 30, 1990 (JESUS) — My dear child, so many of My followers and My disciples have fallen away from Me. They have let the world poison them and so they cannot see Me in simplicity, in the way I visit them and their brothers and sisters. They cannot hear Me because their ears are clogged with the noise of the world. Turn away from material things. Turn to Me, open your hearts! Pray, pray, pray.

My Mother is pleading with you to look towards Heaven. The signs and wonders of your day are there. It is your hearts that I wish to turn gold, and the Miracle of the Rosary is the symbol of that.

(then Our Lady spoke)

My children, do not allow yourselves to be deluded by Satan. Come to me and I will protect you with my garment. Cover yourselves with the prayer of the Rosary. It is a most powerful armor against my adversary. I am calling you because I wish to lead you to my Son and thus you will discover love. Thank you and continue ...

MAY 1, 1990 (JESUS) — My child, do not worry about what is to come. This time has enough in itself. Come to Me with your heart open and you will understand. The world will see war and fire, but this is because of the grave injustices that it commits at this time. The storm to come will purify the earth. It is something worse than mankind has ever seen. Heed My warnings. Listen to what I tell you. I am here for you now and always. At this time My mercy is being shed abundantly upon all of mankind. But the time is soon when My justice will come to cleanse the sin-filled earth. The darkness will then be overtaken by the light and My Mother and I will be victorious. All the world will then live as one with Me. My people, I await your return!

MAY 3, 1990 (JESUS) — My child, the time will soon come upon mankind when justice from the overflowing chalice will pour itself upon the earth. Now, I ask My people to listen to Me, to open themselves to My mercy and to love each other. Now is the time of My mercy ... the time of return. My Mother brings this message to all the world, but so many refuse to listen. They refuse to change. The world is indignant in its sin. My people do not repent. They do not turn to Me. This time of the great mercy will not last forever. Now is when you must choose ... before the great turbulence begins, before you, My people, no longer have so much time. It will come upon you unexpectedly. I do not bring famine, war, and death. I bring love to you. I bring peace to you. The world brings war, death and famine upon itself by sinning. I have given you, My beloved people, free will. You do not need to choose sin; by deciding for God in your days, your lives would be filled with much happiness. Sin brings pleasure for a very short time and a long time worth of misery; just as a life of sin brings an eternity without God, and a life with God, bearing the cross, brings an eternity of bliss with My Father and Me in Heaven.

I am with you at all times. Satan only uses you for his means. That is why sin brings such loneliness, in heart and in mind. But life with Me brings peace in your heart and mind forever. I am with you always.

OPEN YOUR HEARTS

(then Our Lady spoke)

My children, look to the Father in Heaven. Open yourselves to my Son, Jesus. Turn from sin. Turn away from what sin offers you. The devil is at work all over the world and is drowning humanity in iniquity. All of mankind is covered in hate, lies, murder, confusion, and the death of hearts. Pray, my children, for souls who are lost in the great tempest. Pray the Rosary. It is your way to salvation. Call upon me. I am starting the fire which will soon have the world ablaze in the great love of my Son. Begin to love, my darling children. Begin today to decide for God. Live every day with Him. I send you God's peace. Open yourselves. Open your hearts. pray! I love you. Continue ...

MAY 5, 1990 — My children, close yourselves off from the call of the world's evils and temptations. Do not let yourselves be stained by sin. Cover yourselves with my mantle. I will protect you from harm.

MAY 7, 1990 — My dear children, again today I ask you to pray. Pray especially before the crucifix. Pray this prayer:

> **O My loving Jesus, who died for me on the Cross, I thank You with all my heart and I ask for forgiveness for the sins that I committed against You today. Lord Jesus, give me the strength to turn away from temptation and from what Satan offers me, for through Your Most Precious Blood, My Jesus, I am saved.**

My children, please recite this prayer when kneeling before the crucifix. I am physically with you, my children, but soon you will have to live in faith alone. So I ask you to continue to open yourselves to my messages so that you will have a great strength through your faith and so you will have the peace of God with you when it begins. I love you.

MAY 7, 1990 — My child, I wish you to make known all of my requests. I love you my child. Never forget that with God all things are possible. Continue along the path pointed out to you by me. I have hold of your hand and I will not let go. Pray the Rosary every day. Tell all the world to pray, especially this predilected prayer, the Rosary. I send you God's peace.

MAY 8, 1990 — My child, come closer to my heart. Unite yourself with my wishes and live my messages with all your heart. Tell everyone that I wish them to pray more and increase devotion to my Son's Sacred Heart and my Immaculate Heart. Look upon our hearts and understand that my Son and I love each and everyone on the earth. With this increased devotion your hearts will be comforted and graces will come upon you with such abundance! The world must return to God. Mankind must change itself and recognize God. So many people sin with no second thought. Penance has almost disappeared among the minds of the people, including even the faithful. Go to Confession! My children, make reparation for your sins. Pray very much. Return to God. My children, why do you not listen to the call of your loving Mother? Come to me, I await you with open arms.

MAY 9, 1990 — My child, look upon my Son today. He is calling all people in the world to return to God, to return to Him. He has sent His Mother to voice His yearning for souls. He sheds oceans of mercy upon mankind and they are deaf to His plea. My message for today is to pray and live my messages. Open your hearts my children. Open them so that I may begin to work inside of you thus turning your hearts to gold. I wish to turn the earth's stench of sin into a sweet perfume of roses. All of my children, I call on you to listen to me. I call on you to look at the heart of my Son, which is pierced with thorns because of man's great sin. Justice will soon fall upon the world, but its effects can be mitigated through your change.

The chastisement will be much worse if you do not decide for God. If Sodom and Gomorrha would have listened they would have been spared. Today's world is even worse in its sin, so how much worse will the chastisement be! Please, my children, so beloved of my heart, listen! Listen to my voice. Listen and live my messages. I love you.

MAY 14, 1990 — My child, ... all my children, I am asking you with my heart, which is pierced by the sword of sin, to return to God. Jesus is pouring out His love upon you. His mercy is for everyone. Please, come and ask Him to enter your heart, to ease your sufferings. He is calling you through me. His mercy is never-ending; it is so bountiful my little ones; it is so very great. My children, Jesus wishes to make you all into little flowers for the Father. I wish to present you pure to the Eternal Father. My children, only through God can this happen. This is why I ask you to decide for God in everything. Why are you so afraid? You are all so precious to Jesus and yet you turn away from Him. Everything of the earth is passing. Everything of God is eternal. Do not decide for such unneeded things. Turn away from Satan's lures; materialism and television. Be silent, be humble. When you walk with Jesus your lives will be filled with the peace of Heaven. This is everlasting. This is true comfort. The world will not bring you true peace. Only God will give you all that you truly need. My darling ones, decide for God. Open yourselves to Jesus' love and mercy. Be attentive to His call and His wishes. I love you ... continue.

MAY 15, 1990 — My child, I wish to give you the peace of Jesus. I wish to fill your heart with so much love, but you must want this. You must open yourself before Jesus can enter. Pray for souls, pray that I may interact in their lives. Jesus wishes to pour so many graces into your heart, thus making it a furnace of love. Pray for the Holy Spirit and pray to be open to all that Jesus wishes.

JUNE 25, 1990 (JESUS) — My child come to My Mother and Me. Open your heart to us. Immerse yourself in My Sacred Heart and My Mother's Immaculate and Sorrowful Heart. Please, come to us and share in the pains of our hearts. Do you not realize how much I love you? Tonight again you saw the Miracle of the Sun. See how everything turns gold when you look with your eyes afterwards. This is a sign to show you that as you see with your eyes the gold color so I wish your heart to become gold in the love and peace of My Father and Me. My Mother and I are with you always. Continue to pray. Pray the Rosary every day for the special intention of people opening themselves and living the messages when they receive them. Go in My peace.

JUNE 28, 1990 (JESUS) — My child, I have come to you once again today. I have come to ask you to unite your prayers with Me for My children all over the world who have fallen away from Me. Their sins of My denial cause thorns in My heart to pierce Me more, thus causing greater pain. I love them so very much. I am knocking on the door of their hearts but I receive no answer. My child, look upon My Sacred Heart. Feel the pains of My heart. Feel also the burning which is caused by My great love for souls. My children try and run from Me but they cannot. Pray that they return to Me, that I may give them refuge from the world which has caused their sorrow. Pray that they may see that I am the light which can dispel the darkness which surrounds them, thus illuminating their hearts in My love. Pray for My lost children. I await them with open arms.

JUNE 30, 1990 (JESUS) — When you kneel before the Host in adoration you recall My Cross and My Passion and death suffered for humanity. When you kneel before the chalice in adoration you recall My Blood shed for the salvation of all humanity — My blood which wipes away all sins. You, too, recall the blood of the martyrs shed for Christianity. Know then the great importance of the Host, which is My Body, and the chalice, which holds My Precious Blood. Many graces are received from the understanding and the adoration of these two great gifts from God, the Father, to mankind. They represent My great mercy for poor sinners. I call you to compassion and to penance through the Sacrament of the Eucharist. Come to Me, My children, upon whom I wish so much to bestow graces.

* We must remember that Jesus is *TRULY* present in the Most Holy Eucharist from the moment of consecration at the Mass. This is why Our Lord begins speaking about adoration — adoration because of his **TRUE** presence with us in that moment of Consecration at Mass and afterwards.

JULY 28, 1990 (JESUS) — My child, I am calling all the people of the world now to open themselves to My mercy. I am calling every one of My people. I have so much love for them and I only wish peace and happiness for them. Very soon the events which have been foretold to the world will come to pass. Begin to immerse yourselves in a greater way. Begin to understand the great importance of the message I am sending you. Do not wait My people. Soon the great storm will begin. Listen to Me now. Come to Me now, My people, and take refuge. I await your return.

AUGUST 26, 1990 — My child, I am calling you now to seriously open your heart to My Son and me. Please, live the messages which I have been giving to the world. Use the mind that God has given you to fully understand what I am asking through the messages. Pray! Pray that I may lead you into holiness. Pray that my Son may use you in greater ways as an instrument to reach people. Pray especially for souls. Live the messages, my child. Know that I am always with you. I love you.

SEPTEMBER 19, 1990 — My dear children, live the messages that I have been giving you from Heaven. You must begin to live them because now is the time when things will begin to become worse. I am with you, my children, and it is now that I am calling you all to my Son and me. I am calling for you to return to God. Open your hearts, my children. Let God's love and peace fill you. Let Him speak to your heart. He wishes to bring joy into your lives, but you must remain open to Him in good times and in bad. Remember, the crosses He gives are His gifts for you to become holier and for you to grow in His immense love.

Now, my children, is when I am asking you not to delay in living the messages. Time is running out for many because they are putting a deaf ear to Jesus' plea for them to return to Him. He is pouring His mercy upon mankind. Open yourselves to His Love. My children, I, your Mother, am calling you with the words of my Son, "... Return to Me. Do not wait. Return to Me as if you had no time to spare." The times of the great tribulation have arrived. I will protect you with my mantle to cover all of you, whom I love so dearly. Come to me. Let my Son and me bring love to you. Listen to my Son. I love you my children. I love you all with a Mother's love. Listen to the messages I bring. The Father is calling you by name. Return to Him.

Our Lord is calling us to realize the shortness of our lives here on earth and that nothing is worth the loss of eternity. We should live our lives fully focused on Christ; keeping our hearts open to grace.

In the message Our Lady speaks of the "shorteness of time." She wishes for us to understand that every moment is precious and that we should not put God off "until later" but we should respond to Him when we feel His calling, when we hear His voice. At that moment, we should say "yes" to God.

OPEN YOUR HEARTS

SEPTEMBER 20, 1990 (JESUS) — My child ... turn away from the sin that surrounds you. Bring yourself closer to Me. Consecrate more time to Me during your day. Pray! Make prayer a very important part of your day. Many graces will be received from this and you will then grow in the understanding of My love for all of you. You will then know what I ask of you and why. Bear your crosses with humility and obedience. Every cross I give you will only lead you farther along the path of holiness. Return to Me in a greater way every day. Continue to take steps to Me and know that I am always with you.

(then Our Lady began ...)

My dear child, listen to my Son. His words are falling on so many deaf ears. His heart is being pierced by mankind's sins. It hurts Him so to see you continue in your obstinacy of sin.

Look to our hearts, they will give you a secure refuge in this time of the horrible tempest which is destroying faith and which is destroying love between all peoples. I am the Mother of all people and I have come to lead you all back to my Son, Jesus. I have come to lead you back to the Eternal Father. Live the messages I am bringing to you. I love you, my darling ones.

SEPTEMBER 24, 1990 — My child ... tell the world I wish the Rosary to be recited. I wish for the people to contemplate the mysteries so that they will better understand what their Mother and Jesus went through. They will know better by praying and by letting the Holy Spirit fill them with knowledge of the importance of the mysteries.

My children will then realize that I understand their pain and their sufferings. As a Mother, I know my children and I know their sufferings. By praying the Holy Rosary they will better understand this and they will open their hearts more to me, their Mother.

Pray the Rosary. Pray for the Holy Spirit to fill your hearts and minds. Pray, pray, pray, my children. Let prayer be a joy for you. Prayer is such a powerful weapon. Pray the Rosary for protection against Satan, but also so that you will be filled with the Holy Spirit and thus be able to live the messages of the Gospel. My Son is with you. He is calling you to Him. Let Him enter your hearts. I love you, my dear ones.

SEPTEMBER 28, 1990 (JESUS) — Pray very seriously for what is about to come upon mankind for its sins. Humanity is meeting hate with hate and violence with violence. They are ignoring My words.

They are ignoring all that I have given to them and all that I am sending to them now. This is the time of My Divine Mercy. Embrace My love, My children. Look to Me for the answers you seek. You will solve your problems with the love that only I can give. Look to Me in your times of distress. Do not turn to the world for help because it is so contaminated with Satan's darkness.

I am opening My heart for all of you in such abundance. I wish to shed My love upon all of you, but you must open your hearts to receive My love. I will purify you and make of you new vessels to be filled with My love.

Turn to Me, as the time has now come to you. The calamities that I will send will shake the earth, and all of its inhabitants, to its very foundations. Decide for Me now. Decide now, My people.

* The reader should understand that Our Lord is not scolding us in this message. His desire is for us to know the seriousness of His love He says to Michael, "This is the time of My Divine Mercy." In His messages to Blessed Sister Marie Faustina (beatified on Divine Mercy Sunday in Rome, April 18, 1993, by Pope John Paul II) Our Lord says, "Speak to the world of My mercy — it is the sign for the end times; after it will come the Day of Justice," and "... Before the Day of Justice, I am sending the Day of Mercy. I am prolonging the time for the sake of sinners. But woe to them, if they do not recognize this time of My visitation ... While there is still time, let them have recourse to the Fount of My Mercy ... He who refuses to pass through the door of My mercy must pass through the door of My justice."

SEPTEMBER 29, 1990 (JESUS) — My child ... turn away from all other things and pray. I want you to pray! Through prayer your questions will be answered.

Also, pray especially for all that is about to come upon humanity. My people are going to suffer because they have ignored Me. Many souls will be lost and tears will not stop flowing because My people have abandoned their God. They have lost their faith.

Trust in Me, I say to you. Trust in My words. Do you not believe you will receive love and mercy from Me? I love you so much. Why do you continue to turn away? Open your hearts to Me.

Love each other and then you love Me. Love, My children, love must rule in your hearts if there is to be a change. Do not expect things to happen when you do not put trust in Me, your Lord. My people, I am waiting for your return. If only you knew the joy and peace that was awaiting you. You would not spare one minute in returning to Me.

OCTOBER 3, 1990 (JESUS) — The time has now come and so it is important for My people to listen, to begin now to live My messages, the ones I am giving to you through My Mother. Listen well to Her for the words she brings are the truth. My people, return to Me now. Do not waste any more time. You must all become as little children. You must become like them and open your hearts to what I send you. Be open to Me, My people, and realize the great love I have for you. Realize the mercy I am now shedding upon all of you. Open yourselves to all I have to give, My people. Open your hearts to Me, your Lord. I am your Jesus of mercy. I am your Jesus of love. I am yours, My people. Let Me into your homes and your hearts. Let Me guide your lives. Put your trust in Me. I, your Lord, Jesus, will never fail you. Trust in Me, My people. Trust in Me.

OCTOBER 16, 1990 — My child, I call upon you now to increase in fervent prayer and the living of the messages. The world is now beginning the times of which I have been speaking to you. Sin is becoming more manifest in everyday living. It is covering your hearts and your souls with a great darkness, shutting out all good around it. Pray the Rosary. Pray for my intentions and for the plans that I have for you, my children. Look to the Father in Heaven in these times of doubt and uncertainty.

Pray that the Holy Spirit may fill you with wisdom and enlighten you so that you will not be tricked by Satan. Pray, my child, for the times will now become harder for everyone. Do not delay in your everyday conversion.

Return to my Son now! I love you and I am always watching over you. Live the messages. Spread the messages. Open your hearts and let yourselves be filled with the peace that only God can give. Trust in the Lord, my children. Mercy and graces will flow forth upon you all.

OPEN YOUR HEARTS

OCTOBER 18, 1990 — My children, I ask of you this day and every day; conversion: conversion of your hearts. Live the messages. Pray, fast, and do penance, my darling ones. I call you now with great urgency. Return to my Son and do not delay. I love you so very much.

OCTOBER 19, 1990 — My child, ... that soul which opens itself to God does not know nor can it realize the abundance of graces it shall receive. Be open, my child. Pray very much for all of my intentions. I am guarding you from Satan's attacks, but you must know that they will become stronger. Hold tight to my mantle and do not let go for any reason. I am leading you on the path which my Son has chosen for you. Be open to this road and you will be showered with gold from Heaven. I love you, my child, and all of my children in this world. I am always with you.

OCTOBER 28, 1990 — My child, keep your mind on God and on the messages that I have given you. Do not let yourself be taken up by the world in any way. Pray and ask for the Holy Spirit to come down upon you. Pray that God's peace may fill your heart. Only He is able to give true peace. This is why you have not been at ease because you have let worldly things take over your thoughts. Open your heart to God always and in everything that you do. I love you and I am with you always. Know this my child and keep it to heart.

NOVEMBER 1, 1990 FEAST OF ALL SAINTS — My child, lean close to my heart and listen to it whisper of the sweet love of my Son, Jesus. My child, do not fear, my Son, Jesus, and I are with you always. Be strong in your faith and remain in prayer.

NOVEMBER 19, 1990 — My child, continue to open yourself to me. The world is now about to see all that I have been speaking of to many of my children. Come to me in these times. Come to the refuge of my Immaculate Heart. In this garden you will find the calm in the midst of the storm. I love you all, my children.

NOVEMBER 24, 1990 (JESUS) — Let Me come into your heart. Open your heart to Me. Let Me enter into your heart.

DECEMBER 13, 1990 — My children, I am so filled with sorrow and I am now shedding endlessly the tears of my sorrow because humanity is not heeding my call. You, my children, are wasting time. There is not time to waste. I continue to call you and urge you on to conversion, but many of you are still lukewarm to my requests. You must stand strong in this time of darkness. Please, my children, listen to me. This is the last time that I will come to call you to return to God ... the last time, my dear ones. I continue in telling you that there is not much time left at your disposal. My call to conversion is so very urgent, my children. Do not waste time. Take the Rosary in your hands and do not stop praying with it. It is your means of salvation. It is your means of protection against Satan. It is your means of saving souls. Pray, my dear ones, pray!

I leave you in joy and peace in the coming of my Son, Jesus, and in the glorious celebration of Christmas, which is almost here. My children, open your hearts, prepare yourselves spiritually in this time of Advent. Truly celebrate this day of my Son's birth, of Jesus' Light coming into the world. Let your hearts be at peace, my children. I am with you.

DECEMBER 25, 1990 CHRISTMAS DAY — My child, rejoice, for the Son of Man has come into the world. Live in the joy that Jesus brings. Live in the peace that Jesus brings. Live in the light that Jesus brings. Open your hearts to the light of my Son, Jesus. Let your hearts be filled with the immense light that Jesus brings into this world. Be at peace, my children.

DECEMBER 27, 1990 — My child, I call you now to draw ever closer to my Immaculate Heart and to fervently pray. Turn away from the world and from all its offerings. They are poison, which Satan is using to disrupt my plan for you and to contaminate you. You must be strong, carry your cross and do not take your eyes off my Son and me. Open your heart fully now to all that God is pouring upon you. Pray, pray, pray, my child! Do not waste any more time. I love you and I am always with you. Do not fear and do not doubt or be uncertain of anything which comes to your heart from God.

OPEN YOUR HEARTS

MESSAGES FROM THE YEAR 1991

JANUARY 1, 1991 — My child, pray more and more for your brothers and sisters. The year 1991 has come and with it will begin many events to issue in the coming of all of my messages; that which applies to the effects of my messages. Sin will become greater and more widespread throughout the entire world. Satan is very powerful and very active. Pray for all of my intentions, that Satan's plans may be defeated. Decide for God in everything you do. Begin this year by living in the holiness of the messages. Live the messages. Do not waste time, because time is becoming shorter and shorter for all of humanity. You see how your decisions for God have helped in your conversion. Continue along this path. Carry your cross with love. I am with you at all times, so do not be afraid. I love you so very much, my children. Listen to me. Decide for God now.

Our Lady means for us to understand that *she has come with a message of hope; the hope that is Jesus Christ.* She is with us in a particular way because this is an important moment for humanity. If we decide for God then much good will come, but if we ignore God and walk the path of obstinance in our sin, then we will bring great trials upon ourselves. We should realize that Our Lord and His Mother have come to bring light into the darkness of our lives. That every word they speak in the messages is one of love and hope. We absolutely should not focus or dwell on chastisements. If we do, then we have missed the reason for their coming.

JANUARY 8, 1991 — My child, the time has come when I am asking my children to respond to me in the greatest urgency. Do not hesitate and do not waste time. Pray very much, my children, for all of your brothers and sisters who do not believe and are on the road to ruin. My children, turn to me at this time ... please do not refuse my call.

JANUARY 16, 1991 — My dear children, in this time of despair I tell you to open your hearts in a great way and to call upon my Son, ... you will be heard. Live in the peace of God, my dear ones, and do not despair. Peace shall come to the world in time through the glorious triumph of my Immaculate Heart. I love you very much, my children.

JANUARY 22, 1991 — My dear child, the times will become worse for all of the inhabitants of the world because mankind has not listened to my warning and my call. My Son, at this time, wishes only to pour His mercy upon you, but soon will come the time of His justice because of the many sins which offend the Eternal Father. My children, pray and make reparation for the many offenses against my Son, Jesus Christ. The events dealing with the warnings and the chastisements, which I have told some of my children, will soon come upon the earth. Prepare yourselves, my children, by prayer, fasting, and a renunciation of this world. My dear children, listen to me and respond to my call! The destruction you are seeing in the world at this time is Satan's work. You can defeat him in your lives through prayer and fasting. My little ones, pray every day, especially that most predilected prayer of mine, the Holy Rosary.

FEBRUARY 1, 1991 (JESUS) — My people, open your hearts to Me. At this time I wish to shed innumerable amounts of graces upon you. This is why I now again send My Mother to you. She comes bringing My words. Please, do not deny Me this wish, that I may fill your hearts with the true joy and peace of heaven. Let Me enter into your hearts so that I may make of you new and blossoming golden roses.

FEBRUARY 8, 1991 — My dear child, I urgently call upon you to pray everyday, to make prayer a very important part of your life and not to neglect it. Especially, I ask of you the prayer of the Most Holy Rosary. Recite it every day. My message is ever so urgent, my children. Please listen to me and do not refuse my call.

FEBRUARY 8, 1991 SECOND MESSAGE — My child, tell all the world of my messages. Tell the world of my motherly presence among you. Do not be afraid, for I will protect you with my immaculate light, which will blind your enemies and will scare away the demons. My mantle will be your protection against Satan. Put on the cloak of my light through prayer, fasting, reparation, and a renunciation of this sin-filled world. Ignore the slurring and errant voice of the world, which slanders and spreads lies against My Son and against the Holy Catholic Church. Have complete and unbending faith in my messages to you for they are the same in all the world. I come to the earth for the last time to call all of my children back to the path of God, back to the path which leads to true peace and joy and which leads to eternity in Heaven. I come with the words of my Son, "Return to Me, My people." I am your Immaculate Mother. Call upon me, my children. I will protect you in the storm. I will guard your lives with the power given to me by the Most Holy Trinity. I come to lead humanity, so blackened with the stain of sin, back to my Son, Jesus Christ. Listen to my voice, my children. Listen, for your souls are at stake. I love you and I bless you with my motherly presence.

FEBRUARY 11, 1991 — My child, feel the comfort and the peace that surrounds you during the prayer of the Rosary. Pray the Rosary every day. Give time to the Rosary. All problems and all troublesome situations will be given answers through the power of the Most Holy Rosary. I am with you when you pray it. The Rosary will bring the sweet fragrance of roses into your lives and into your souls. It will aid you greatly on your path to God. Pray it devoutly. It is your protection. It is your gift from Heaven given through me, your Blessed Mother. I love you and I ask you to hold onto it with all of your strength and to never stop praying it. It brings great graces, my children.

FEBRUARY 13, 1991 – ASH WEDNESDAY — My child, remain ever so close to my Immaculate and Sorrowful Heart. The smell of roses around you is my sign that I am with you. So, I wish you to not have any fear. Call upon me in your times of trouble. I love you, my child. Continue to pray for my intentions.

MARCH 3, 1991 — My dear child, continue to immerse yourself in prayer. Pray the Rosary every day as I have asked you, as I have asked the entire world to do. Continue to tell all those around you, all my children, to pray the Holy Rosary every day because many graces are given through the Rosary. Pray continuously. My message is urgent to all of mankind. Repent and sin no more because God is greatly offended. The chalice is running over with the sins of man. Pray, pray, pray. I love you all my dear children.

MARCH 8, 1991 — My child, tell all of my children of the messages which I have been giving you. Tell the world to reconcile itself with

God quickly, as the time is near when the events, which I have told some of my children, will come. My Son now sends His mercy upon the world. Tell my children to open themselves to my Son's Divine Mercy. Continue to pray the Rosary. Tell the world to pray from the heart. Open your hearts to God, my children. I love you and I bless you In the Name of the Father, and of the Son and of the Holy Spirit. Go in peace.

MARCH 20, 1991 — My child, embrace the Cross. Embrace the prayer of the Rosary and look upon me, into the eyes of your Mother, and feel the warmth of my arms enwrapping your soul. In this way you will find peace. Return to the Rosary. It is your sure guide in this bitterly cold world.

MARCH 29, 1991 – GOOD FRIDAY — Behold, my child, Jesus on the Cross and the agony which He suffered through for all of mankind's sins. Behold the nails piercing both His hands and His feet and the crown of thorns on His head. Open your hearts to my Son. Open your hearts and join with me in asking my Son for mercy upon the world. Open your hearts and your eyes and behold my Son, Jesus, in redemption on the Cross for the sins of the world. Pray and unite yourself through meditation on the Passion of Jesus. My children, pray!

MARCH 31, 1991 – EASTER SUNDAY — Come, my dear children, and rejoice with me, for my Son, the Savior of the World, has risen from the dead. Through His death on the Cross and His resurrection He has saved the world. My children, open your hearts to the fullness of this day. Rejoice in the Lord!

APRIL 1, 1991 — My dear children, realize the urgency of my messages. Realize, also, the importance of my requests, that you pray the Rosary frequently and that you unite yourselves in prayer with my Son. Pray, my dear children, pray.

APRIL 2, 1991 (JESUS) — Tell My people to pray often, to pray the Rosary in union with My Mother and to offer up their prayers to ease the pains of My Mother's Sorrowful Heart. Tell the world that the time left is short. Listen to My voice. Let those who can hear, hear Me, and those who can see, see Me, through the miracles that are becoming manifest through the belief in Me and in My Mother's appearances all over the world. Come to Me, My people, come. I await you with open arms.

APRIL 7, 1991 – FEAST OF DIVINE MERCY— My dear child, tell all the world of the great mercy of my Son, Jesus. Today, on this the Feast of Divine Mercy, my Son overwhelmingly sheds His mercy upon all of humanity. Open your hearts to the love, compassion and mercy of Jesus. Open your heart and pray, my children, pray. Let Jesus fill your hearts with His great love and mercy. Go in the peace of God.

APRIL 11, 1991 — My dear child, I call upon you to remain ever so close to my Immaculate Heart. In these days when Satan is taking so many souls away from my Son and me, I ask you to pray fervently for the conversion of sinners and for unbelievers. Have faith, my child. Be strong and remain close to the light of my Son, Jesus. He sends me to bring you all back to His way, for He is the way, the truth, and the life. Look to Heaven, my dear ones. God is granting graces beyond imagination to all the world at this time. Listen to the messages which I bring to you from Heaven. I, your Mother, call upon you to live the message of the Gospel — to pray, do penance, and live in mortification. This will help you on your path of life. This will help you to destroy the darkness. My dear children, I come bringing hope. I love you.

APRIL 30, 1991 — My dear child, it has been some time since I have given you a message. This is because I have wanted you to pray and to grow in the messages I have already given to you. A Mother teaches her children slowly. I wish you to first learn to walk before you try to run. Please, continue to pray the Rosary every day for peace in the world and for unbelievers. Continue also to spread the messages which I am giving the world. Tell everyone of my messages. Pray and remain ever close to my Immaculate Heart. Continue on the road which I have set for you. Pray also before the crucifix for the conversion of sinners and for all of my intentions. I love you and I am with you always. Go in God's peace.

MAY 2, 1991 — My dear child, I ask you to pray every day so that you can grow in the fullness of God's love for you ... so that you can grow in my love for you. Your prayer makes you stronger against Satan's attacks and against all temptations, which come from him. My child, I ask you and all the world to pray, especially the Rosary, every day for the conversion of sinners and to obtain peace in the world — peace which can only come from God. My child, I ask you also to fast strictly, as I have asked in Medjugorje, on Wednesdays and Fridays on bread and water alone. Know that fasting is pertinent to prayer and the graces received from both. Do penance, also, for your sins and the sins of those around you.

Go to Confession frequently and also go to Holy Mass as often as you can. Please, my child, do as I ask and please my heart so much in doing so. I am the Lady of the Rosary. I am the Lady of the Roses. I am the Mother of All Mankind. Tell the world of my messages. Do not be afraid, my child. Be strong in the Lord and pray for the Holy Spirit to fill you. Nothing more is needed for peace on earth. Nothing more but God and all that He asks. Again, tell the world of my messages. Tell the world to convert now. The time before the great events is now so very short. Tell my children to pray and repent now. Go in the peace of God. I love you, my child.

MAY 13, 1991 — My child, my dear one, listen to me. My child, know that my Son is calling you. Tell everyone of the words that I have given you. Spread the messages and do not be afraid. I love you and so you should not fear.

MAY 23, 1991 My dear child, I ask you to pray the Rosary. Come close to my Immaculate Heart. Be a light to those around you. Live my Son's words, which are contained in the Gospels. Live in my Son. Live love and mercy every day of your life. Pray every day! Thank the Father for everything which He has given to each of you in your lives. Thank my Son for the great mercy which He is pouring upon the world. My child, pray. Prayer will clear your mind. Prayer will cleanse the wounds which come from the poisoned and diseased world. Pray every day and cover yourself in the perfume of roses, the perfume of my protection. Where the Rosary is prayed I, my child, am present. Spread the Good News. Tell the world of the great grace which has descended upon the world. Tell it and **LIVE** it.

JUNE 4, 1991 — My child, be a strong and silent apostle. Live the messages and by doing so be a light to those around you. Hold strong to the faith. Consecrate a period of time each day to the Immaculate Heart of your Mother. Continue to pray the Holy Rosary, so beloved of my heart. With it countless souls can be saved. Pray, my child ... for mankind is running out of time. It must heed the call with which I have come down from Heaven. My dear children, please, hear the voice of your Mother and repent of your sins. I call you all most urgently. The chastisement is about to befall the world. It is not too late to make reparation and to mitigate the horror of the purification, but you must listen to my voice. My dear children, pray! Pray every day and live with your whole heart the message that I have brought to you in so many parts of the world. Do you not see that it is more urgent that you listen now? More than ever mankind is enclosed in a great darkness. Sin is lived within lives without thought to morals or what is right and wrong. I have come to the world bringing the light and salvation of my Son, Jesus Christ. His mercy is never-ending. Open your hearts to Him, my children. Call upon the Name of the Lord. Open your hearts. I am with you and with the angels in Heaven I am protecting you. I love you, my children.

JUNE 12, 1991 — My child, I urge you greatly to tell those around you that I am calling the world urgently. You should not waste time. Inform them of the urgency of my messages. Live the messages with your heart. So many people are lukewarm because they have not said "yes" to God. They have chosen their own path. Even those souls who are chosen by Him have gone back to old habits of not praying or fasting. I tell you, my children, listen now and live the messages with seriousness. The time to change is now, do not wait. Time is precious. Use every minute to live the Gospel of Jesus. Thank you, my children, for helping me. I am with you in these terrible times. I love you, my little ones.

JULY 10, 1991 — Tell all my children that the time before the chastisement is now so very short. Tell the world to listen to my messages. People must begin to pray and do penance. Fast, my children!

JULY 15, 1991 (JESUS) — Offer Me every suffering, even if it is little. Offer also every trial to Me.

AUGUST 12, 1991 — My children, do not concentrate on the negative things. Put emphasis on that which is positive.

AUGUST 18, 1991 My dear child, I do not need to give you any more messages. Everything that you need to keep your faith strong and to have the peace of God in your hearts has been given to you. You need only to live the messages. The messages given to you are the same all around the world. Pray every day, my dear ones. Go to Confession often to ask Jesus for pardon of your sins, which greatly afflict our hearts.

Receive the Body and Blood of my Son, Jesus, truly present in the Holy Sacrifice of the Mass. Mortify yourselves and repent of your sins. God will grant the world mercy through the Cross. Pray to God that He may grant forgiveness and lessen the punishments. I am with you always ... always. Keep me in your hearts. I love you so very much, my dear children. Please me by living my messages and by reciting the Holy Rosary often. I leave you now in the peace of God. Go and walk firmly in your faith. I will be with you at all times.

My child, fear not and spread my messages. The world must know that it is in grave danger. The world must return to the Lord. It must return now! Do not wait. You have but a very short time. Listen to my voice, my children. Listen and believe in those who tell you of my messages, for they tell the truth and I am with them.

* Our Lady, when referring to time being short, does not necessarily mean 6 months or 2 years, but a "time" that could be 5, 8, or 10 years (or more). This is why, even though her messages are very serious in her calling us to realize the importance of time, she does not mean for us to panic and believe that her reason for coming is only to warn us. Our Lady has said that there is a danger for the world if we do not respond to the graces we are being given, but our response should always be one of hope and joy; one of love and mercy. God will take care of the rest. Fear and worry should not be in our hearts.

OCTOBER 3, 1991 — The time will come soon when I will ask you to spread the messages that you have received. You must remain strong. My Son and I will give you great strength with which to be strong in your faith and in your testimony of my messages to you and to the world. You will not bend in the great storm of unfaithfulness to my call. Satan will use everything to weaken my chosen souls, but he will not succeed in conquering the Catholic Church. My Son prophesied this almost two thousand years ago when He said that not even the Gates of Hell would prevail against the Church. Spread my messages. Tell my children that they must open their hearts and have great faith in my Son and me in the coming times. I will not be with you much longer and so I urgently call upon all of you who have opened your hearts to double your efforts in your prayer and in your actions. Be a living testimony to my messages, to my Son's words, to the Gospels. Pray from your heart, my child, and let the seed of my message, of my Son's light, blossom and become a brilliant and beautiful flower of virtue and of faith. Pray, my children, please pray. Prayer is especially needed in these times of yours. Do not have any fear, my little ones. I am with you and I am protecting you at every moment on every step of your journey.

OCTOBER 7, 1991 – FEAST OF THE HOLY ROSARY — My dear child, I am the Woman of the Apocalypse. I am the Woman of the New Times, which are on the verge of coming to this world, so filled with the darkness of sin. My child, pray continuously for the completion and fulfillment of the plan of salvation for all the human race. The world has but run out of time. It does not even realize that it is at the abyss. My children sin without thought to the damage they do to those around them and the damage they do to their souls. They are on the path to Hell. I call my children, all people of the world, to listen to my voice with simplicity and humility and to heed my call for conversion. Hearts must open themselves in reparation. I am calling all hearts to open themselves to Jesus so that they may be filled with His Divine Mercy, His Divine Love. My children, all of humanity, please listen to the voice of your Heavenly Mother. Tears fall from my eyes to cleanse you; tears of sorrow and tears of joy. Tears of sorrow, because I see the great sin of the world, but tears of joy, because the time of the Triumph of my Immaculate Heart is about to come upon the world.

NOVEMBER 8, 1991 — Do not have any fear ... I am with you. Continue along the path which your heart leads you, for it is I who leads you.

NOVEMBER 14, 1991 — My dear child, why do you let doubt, fear and worry seep into your heart, thus filling yourself with a lack of faith and discontentment. Do you know that I have been with you all this time? It is I, your Mother, who speaks to you from Heaven. She wishes you to know that she loves you very much and that she is with you and will never abandon you. Do not let your faith grow weak, but open your heart to the fullness of the Lord and the love and mercy that He wishes to bestow upon you. Prepare for the year that is to come with penance, prayer and sacrifice. My adversary wishes to thwart my plans. Pray very much so that he will not succeed. My children, I am with you always. Be comforted and believe in my messages to you. Be strong in your faith and in the Lord. Jesus is with you. Open your hearts, my dear children, and accept my messages with warmth and sincerity. Be docile, my children, and follow your Mother with love. She is leading you to her Son, Jesus. I love you, my precious ones. Pray, pray, pray for the Holy Spirit to enkindle the flame of love in your hearts.

NOVEMBER 18, 1991 — My dear child, continue along the path which I, your Mother, am leading you. Immerse yourself into the depths of my heart and pray, my child, pray. I am calling on all those who have heard my voice to pray. Prayer is especially needed at this time in the world. My child, do not have any fear of what is to come. I am with you and I will continue to protect you. The tempest ahead will be very rough for humanity, but for those who listen to my call my special protection will assist them in their times of need. Do not forget, I am a merciful Mother and I wish to be called upon in your times of distress so that I, your Mother, can help you. I am taking your prayers my children, and am placing them before my Son, so that the chastisements may be lessened. God's hand of justice weighs heavy upon the world at this time and so I ask you to pray to lessen that which is to come. Do not forget that I love you and that I, your Mother, will always be with you. I will especially assist you in the times that are to come. Be strong in your faith and live in the love of my Son, Jesus. Invoke constantly the names of Jesus and Mary. I love you, my precious children. Do not forget that I am with you.

NOVEMBER 30, 1991 — My dear child, I am calling you to constant prayer at this time when it is so needed. My children, during this season of Advent I am calling you to mortification of the senses and reparation for your purification and for the conversion of sinners. I wish to bring all of you to my Son's heart during this season in preparation for His glorious coming at Christmas. My Son comes to enlighten all the world and He wishes to fill your hearts with light and so for this you must be open. Again, my children, I ask you to open your hearts to the love and mercy of my Son, Jesus, so that He may fill you with a desire to do His will and to be at peace during this season of Advent. For this to happen, my children, you must pray and fast. Then will your hearts be purified so that I may present your hearts to the Sacred and Merciful Heart of Jesus. My children, open your hearts to my call. I am with you and I wish to present and give to you the love and peace of my Son. Be open, my children, and prepare for Christmas with prayer and with acts of love and reparation.

DECEMBER 2, 1991 — My dear child, I am calling upon you to open your heart. All of my children, please listen to my call with open hearts. Open yourself to the will of God, to what He wishes, so that your hearts may be aflame with the Holy Spirit and a love for my Son. My dear ones, I have been with you for so long and my messages remain the same; return to my Son, return to the ways of God. For this end, pray, fast, and do penance. Be humble and loving in all of your actions. Do not fear, my dear ones, when Satan attacks you because you are doing God's bidding; rather, have faith that I, your Mother, am protecting you with my mantle of love. I am interceding for you before the Father. I, your Mother, am keeping constant watch over you, my precious ones. I love you and I am with you.

Do not fear, then, and do not worry. Live with a strong faith in my Son and know that He is protecting your work. Continue, my children, along the path of my Jesus. Continue to carry your crosses with love and with patience. My children, I am blessing and protecting you at every moment along your long journey. Please, continue to pray that my plans may come to pass. Continue to hold the Cross close to your heart. Continue to pray and prepare for the coming of Jesus. Pray, my children, pray for the strength to do the will of God in all things. Pray for peace in the world. Pray, my dear ones, pray in all things and at all times. Prayer is your sure guide in your times of temptation and trouble. Prayer, my children, is your light in the darkness. Prayer can answer all of your problems. Open your hearts to the mercy of Jesus through prayer. My children, pray always. Prayer, my children, is your weapon against Satan and your sure path to paradise. Do not abandon prayer and do not forget prayer in this trial which you are living through. Especially, my children, do not forget the prayer of the Rosary, your way to saving souls and to shackling the dragon. Let the Rosary be your symbol of life and comfort. Let it encircle you with graces. Let it be a key to your relationship with my Jesus. My children, in the great trial which is ever increasing in its horror, I am calling you to prayer and to the sacraments. Employ these weapons to strengthen your families and yourselves. My children, adore the Holy Eucharist in which my Son is present for all humanity. Graces abound from this sacrament. My children, grow to let the Holy Mass and the Eucharist be your life's center so that Jesus may be at the center of your hearts and your lives. Walk with my Son with these; prayer and the Sacraments.

My children, I have come to lead you to my Son, Jesus Christ, the Savior of all humanity. My children, open your hearts to Him, for He is the light that will enkindle everlasting peace in your hearts. Jesus awaits you. My Son knocks at the doors of your hearts; my children, open them. Please, listen to this Mother. I love you all, my children, and I, your Mother, am with you.

DECEMBER 12, 1991 — My dear children, I am calling you to continue to spend this Advent in prayer and in expectation of the coming of my Son, Jesus, at Christmas. Open yourselves to the peace and joy that only God can give. Open yourselves to Jesus and live my Son's message of love and peace during this time. My dear children, I am with you and I continue to call you to peace and to reconciliation in your hearts. For this I ask you to go to Confession to ask God for forgiveness of your sins so that your hearts may be pure for my Son. Also, my dear ones, forgive those around you for their offenses against you. Live the love of Jesus and act as He did on earth, my children. I call you to forgive through love; then the peace of Jesus will enter into all of your hearts during this season of Advent. It is especially important for reconciliation and peace within the family. My children, do not let Satan cause disruptions in your hearts and in your families. Fight his presence with prayer and penance. In this way you will be able to be more open to my Jesus and to His message of peace. My children, be reconciled with one another. Love is the key to your victory over Satan and his chains of disagreement.

My children, I call you especially to realize that my Son and I are with you always. Let the seeds of peace grow in your hearts through love. My children, love one another and be a reflection of my Son, Jesus, every day of your life. Take up your crosses with love. Forgive with love. Act with love. Pray with love focused in your heart. To love, my children, is to know Jesus. Do not forget this when others do harm to you; instead, forgive them and make peace within your heart and with those around you. God will bless you for it. My children, let this season of Advent be one of love, peace and reconciliation. I love you, my children, and I, your Mother, am with you.

DECEMBER 21, 1991 — My dear children, continue along the path which I have made for you. Continue, my children, to open your hearts to the Lord, Who is coming in glory. My dear children, open yourselves to celebrate with love, joy and peace the birth of my Son, Jesus, the birth of the Savior of the World. Continue to prepare for His coming, my children, ... both the spiritual coming at Christmas, celebrating His physical descent to the world and also, my children, prepare the seed of love and hope for His coming the second time. My children, pray with me at this time for peace in the world and for the Triumph of my Immaculate Heart. I am calling all of you, my children, to respond with open hearts and with love. My children, please do not abandon me at this time.

The world is at a crucial point and you, my children, can help to defeat the work of the evil one in the world, through your prayers and sacrifices. My children, I call you to prepare for this new year with much prayer and many sacrifices and to continue to be open to the will of the Lord. My children, I bless you with the peace of Heaven. My children, open your hearts to the Child who fills this darkened world with never-ending light. Open your hearts to the coming of my Son, Jesus, at Christmas. My children, live the messages that I give to you. I am with you, my precious ones, always.

DECEMBER 23, 1991 — My dear child, my Son wishes to bring light to this world so darkened by hate and greed, by sin, my children. My Son, Jesus, is calling all of humanity to open itself to Him, to His heart, to His never-ending mercy. My dear ones, I, your Mother, am calling you to pray very much at this time that the people of the world will listen to my call and will answer with open hearts. My children, humanity is on the verge of great calamities. The world must return to God, the Father. I, my children, am calling you for the last time. My message remains the same; pray, do penance, live peace, and make reparation for the offenses against the Sacred Heart of my Son and against the Father in Heaven. My children, open yourselves to the power of the Holy Spirit. Do not doubt in the wonders that the Holy Spirit can bring you if you have faith. My children, I say it again, have faith and believe. I am with you. Do not doubt, my little ones, but open your hearts to the message I bring, ... I love you and I am with you at all times. Prepare, my children, for what is to come. Prepare through prayer and fasting. Prepare through obedience to my Son. Prepare with a love for your neighbor. Cultivate the message I bring to you with joy and with a love for my Son and me. My children, I love you so very much. I am with you. Be at peace, my children. Open yourselves to the spirit of Christmas, to the coming of my Son; the Light of the World, the Prince of Peace.

OPEN YOUR HEARTS

MESSAGES FROM THE YEAR 1992

JANUARY 7, 1992 — My dear child, I am calling all of humanity to open itself to the Lord and to prepare with my messages for what God will send upon the earth. My children, I call you ever so urgently to pray, fast, and make reparation for your sins. My children, be prepared for the warnings and for the chastisement. My children, I love you and I will not abandon you in your time of need, but I pray for you to be able to open yourselves to my Son's mercy and to be prepared for the trial that even now you are on the edge of living through. My children, once again I say to you, ... open your heart to Jesus, my Son. Open your hearts to this Mother who calls you with a burning desire for you to be purified so that I may present your prayers before the Lord for the salvation of souls. My child, tell everyone to pray especially at this time for those souls who do not know my Son and for those who refuse to open themselves to Him. Wait and watch in prayer. I am with you, my children.

JANUARY 13, 1992 — My dear child, the times that you and your brethren are living through are the last times. I have come from Heaven, my children, to call all of mankind back to the ways of God. My children, I seriously call upon you to decide for my Son, Jesus Christ. My children, open your hearts in prayer. The times you live in are very dangerous and if mankind does not decide for God then the chastisement will come and the punishment for the world's sins will be beyond imagination. My children, I do not say this to cause fear but to warn you again of the imminent danger all of mankind is in. My children, again, I ask you to listen to my voice, the voice of your loving Mother. I love you all, my children. Please respond to my call with open hearts and with love. I am your Mother.

JANUARY 13, 1992 - SECOND MESSAGE — My dear child, I ask you to pray fervently for all the souls in Purgatory who suffer for the final expiation of their sins. They will enter Heaven, but with your prayers they will be able to enter eternal happiness in Paradise much sooner. My children, pray, ... pray very much for the souls in Purgatory. Offer up at least one Rosary a week for these precious souls. My children, offer up each prayer with the Precious Blood of my Son for these souls.

45

My children, have faith and pray. Ease the sufferings of our hearts through your prayer and sacrifices. My children, as always, I call upon you, who have heard my call, to pray and fast with serious intention to make amendment for your sins and the sins of mankind. I suffer greatly because I am the Mother of All Mankind. My children, if you only knew the great stench of sin that rises from the earth. My children, you live in very dark times. Open your hearts to the light of my Son. Open your hearts and pray for those souls who do not know my Son. Pray especially for unbelievers, for the conversion of sinners, for the youth, for those souls who are lukewarm in responding to my love, and most especially I call you to pray and make reparation for the sin of abortion.

The devil's grip strengthens with those who believe in and practice this horrible atrocity against the Father's gift of life. The abyss for those souls is so very deep. Pray very much, my children, for those souls connected with this sin. I am with you and I bless you in the Name of the Father, and the Son, and Holy Spirit. Pray, my children, pray. This is my message to you this day.

JANUARY 13, 1992 - THIRD MESSAGE — My child, tell my children that I wish that they not refuse the belief in Purgatory. This place of suffering is real. The souls in Purgatory are in great need of your prayers. Have pity on them. Show mercy on them by praying for them and by asking my Son to pour endless drops of His Precious Blood upon them to ease their sufferings. Pray for the dead, my children. I leave you now in God's peace.

JANUARY 15, 1992 — My dear children, please do not be deceived by Satan. He is disguising his movements in his darkness and in his cloud of immorality. My children, open your hearts to me. I have come to lead you all back to My Son, the Light of the World, Jesus Christ. My children, you will better be able to open yourselves to the path I ask you to follow if you pray and fast. Pray especially, my children, the Rosary. Meditate on the events of My Son's life. My children, again I say, open your hearts and accept the light that I bring. Place the seed of love, of My Son, in your hearts and let the light of peace and love grow in your lives and in the world. My children, pray very much for my intentions. Satan at this time is very active and wishes to destroy my plans. Pray and call upon the angels for your protection. I am with you.

** Our Lady let me understand that Satan hides himself in the darkness of immorality. This is twofold in that he wants us to fall into this darkness and confusion thinking that we are not sinning and also to reach his final aim, that is to take the soul to Hell with him. He is succeeding in making immorality seem like it is not sin. This leads many people to sin against God, especially against the 6th Commandment. These souls are then led by Satan down this path and into Hell. This is why Our Lady continually calls us to decide for God, to choose to follow God and to turn away from sin when Satan presents temptations to us.**

JANUARY 18, 1992 — My dear child, inform the world that it is in very great danger. This is why, again, I have come to warn you and also to call you to prayer and penance. My children, please make many sacrifices to ease the sufferings of our hearts and to lessen the chastisements. My children, pray also and make sacrifices for the world. My children are immersed in the darkness of sin. Please hear and respond to my call.

JANUARY 19, 1992 — My dear children, once again, I am calling you to take time out of your day to pray. My children, the wrath of God will come upon the earth but you can lessen its effects with your continuous prayer and fasting. I pray for you all, my children, that you respond to my call and to my requests without hesitation and with the greatest urgency. I say to you, please do not waste the time that has been given you from above. It (time) is for your conversion. Again, do not wait to see how the world will respond to what will occur. Each of you, my children, is first responsible for yourself. Pray and open your hearts to My Son and to me, Your Mother. I will guide you and protect you in your times of difficulty and confusion. Do not be alarmed if some of my messages seem harsh or severe; it is only to warn you and to help you realize the urgency needed in your response. Go now in peace, my dear ones. I am forever your Mother and I will always be with you.

Then a special message was given for the locutionist:

I will guard you against all attacks and My Son will protect and bless you in your journey and mission. Go in my love and with the protection of My Son. May the Holy Spirit descend upon you and all those with you.

JANUARY 20, 1992 — My dear children, purify your hearts through prayer and fasting. I call you to a greater realization and understanding of my messages and to the importance of them. My children, I continue to come again and again in so many different places to call you back to God; to call you back to My Son, Who is love and Who wishes to pour His mercy upon you. I love you, my children. I again call you to change; to decide for God in everything, to put God in the first place, my children, and not to be preoccupied with the things of the world. Turn to me, Your Mother. I love you and I will lead you all to My Son and to the glory of Heaven. My children, continue to take steps on the paths of conversion, penance, fasting, mortification, and prayer. Do not let those around you who disbelieve discourage you. Have a strong faith. I, Your Mother, will guard you at every step. I love you, my children. Do not forget this, especially in your times of need. I am with you. My children, do you not realize the importance of my messages? Do not waste even a moment in your return to the Father. I am leading you. I am the Mother of All Mankind. Please, listen to my call and respond with open and sincere hearts.

JANUARY 21, 1992 — My dear children, come one and all back to the Father. You, my children, must help one another through your prayers and through your actions of charity and love. Pray the Rosary, my children, with one another in mind. Save souls through your humble and sincere response to my call. I am your Mother of love and I wish for you to open yourselves to the love and mercy of My Son, Who shed His blood on the Cross for the salvation of all the world. My children, respond with love. Thank you for opening your hearts. Thank you, my children, for your response of love. I will continue to carry you in my heart. Do not fear over what is to come. I will be with you in the hard times ahead of you. Love and live in the light of My Son, Jesus. Thank you, my children.

JANUARY 21, 1992 - SECOND MESSAGE — My children, you have forgotten how to be humble. Love and forgive. Forgive, my children, as my Son forgave. Love one another. Do not make excuses, my little ones. Open your hearts and love and ask for forgiveness for your sins. My Son will pardon you in your sincerity for mercy. My children, I love you. I am your Queen of Heaven. I ask you to place yourselves in the protection of My Immaculate Heart for peace and so that I may guard you against attacks. Again, my little ones, pray and do not let Satan seduce you into sin. Open yourselves fully to my call. Pray very much for yourselves so that you may be prepared for what is to come. I will guide you along your paths. I am with you at every rocky step. I love you all, my dear and beloved children. Return to My Son. He calls upon you to love and open yourselves to His merciful heart. Do not turn away from Him, I beg you, my children. Be open in prayer and accept with love and humility my call of love. I am with you.

JANUARY 29, 1992 — My dear children, once again I call you to prayer and sacrifice. Many will perish in the flame of the purification because they have not responded to my call, because they have refused to listen ... they have refused to love. My children, open yourselves to my messages with prayer. Open yourselves with fasting. My children, I call you urgently to respond. In this year in a greater way the battle will continue between myself and my adversary, the Dragon. Pray, my children, that those who have turned away from the Lord will again open themselves and return to Him. My Son awaits you all with love and mercy. I love you, my children, and I am watching over you and protecting you.

JANUARY 31, 1992 — You, my beloved children of the world, are at the edge of the abyss. You are ready to put yourselves into the hands of my adversary, Satan. You, my children, should realize that you are living through the decisive times of the battle. To choose for evil, for Satan, is to choose against My Son. You, my children, are walking toward Hell. You are walking with Satan while you sin. My children, I call you again to turn away from the world and from the great sea of sin that man is drowning in. You, my beloved little ones, are being poisoned in the sea of immorality and filth that is propagated and spread through words and actions. My children, consecrate yourselves to me so that I may, in a greater way, protect you by placing you under my mantle. My children, call upon the angels for protection. Call especially upon St. Michael, who is leading the angels in battle against

Satan. My dear children, pray also for your further conversion and for your strength during these times. Pray, my children, that you will not be put to the test. My children, love one another. Reconcile yourselves with God and with one another. My children, listen to me, your Mother. I have come to lead you back to My Son. Listen and respond.

JANUARY 31, 1992 - SECOND MESSAGE — My dear children, why do you wait to return to My Son? I am pleading with all of humanity to open itself to my call for conversion. My children, my words are the same to you. Please, open your hearts. Do not continue along the road of sin, along the road of ruin. My little ones, please my heart and return to the Father in Heaven. Please my heart, give me great joy, my children, by praying the Rosary with love and with faith everyday. In this way I will defeat Satan at every step and then my plans can be fully realized. I wish to save the greatest number of souls. I love you all, my children. Do not forget that in the time to come. Know that I will not abandon you.

FEBRUARY 3, 1992 — My children, do not think that because I appeared many years ago in Fatima that my messages given there are not relevant. My children, my messages given there are more important now than ever before. Continually pray, fast, sacrifice, and make reparation for the sins which continue to offend my heart and the Sacred Heart of My Son. My children, the cup is overflowing. Pray for the unbelievers. If the world continues on its path of ruin and does not change soon, then the chastisements will come. I bless you all and I am with you.

FEBRUARY 6, 1992 — I am the Mother of All Mankind. I am with you and have been with you. I will always be with you. My children, please, pray with open and sincere hearts. Pray the Rosary especially for the souls who continue to sin and to cause atrocities of sin, in ignorance of the faith and of God. I call you to fast also and to unite your prayers and fasts with the sufferings of My Immaculate Heart. I call you to pray with serious intention, to continue on your path of conversion and be courageous in spreading this serious message. The world is at the edge. If mankind does not change its ways and return to the Father then it will perish in the purification that is on the verge of coming to you. I love you, my children. Please, listen to my call and respond to me, Your Mother, with love and sincerity.

FEBRUARY 7, 1992 — My dear child, write ... My children, I call you again to pray seriously for my lost children who stand at the abyss of death eternal. My child, many of my priest sons are in grave danger, for they have fallen away from My Son and from the Holy Father. Pray, pray, my children, for these souls who are lost in the darkness, which now covers the earth. My children, respond to me with love. I love you and I am with you.

FEBRUARY 7, 1992 – SECOND MESSAGE (During Exposition) — My dear child, pray for the numerous souls who are on the road to Hell. Pray that they may change and return to the Father. I am with you and I love you.

FEBRUARY 9, 1992 — My dear child, write what I wish to convey to the world. My children, I am your Sorrowful Mother. I am in great sorrow because you, my beloved ones, are not opening your hearts. You, my children, continue to disobey the laws of God. You, my children, continue in your obstinacy of sin. My beloved children, do you not realize the times that you are in? Do you not realize that the future of the world hangs by a thread. My children, I love you all so very much. This is why my tears are now never ending. I call you ever so urgently to pray and to make sacrifices, to call upon the Holy Spirit to descend and fill your hearts. I call you all to return to my motherly protection so that I may, in turn, bring you all to My Son, Jesus Christ. My Son awaits humanity with great mercy. Do not ignore His call. Do not turn away from our love. My children, respond with love and with open hearts. I am your Mother. I am the Mother of All Mankind. I call you to return to the Father. Listen intently, my children, and respond.

FEBRUARY 19, 1992 — My dear child, please write all that I tell you. My children, this day I call you seriously to change, to seriously decide for God, to decide against sin, to turn away from temptation. All my children, I love you so much, this is why my messages to you are urgent and serious. You, my children, beloved of my heart, I tell you the events are about to begin. These events I have revealed to a few of my chosen children. My children, prepare by praying and fasting. My children, make sacrifices for your sins. Pray for the Holy Spirit to descend upon you and fill your hearts with a burning desire to follow God and His laws of love. My children, turn away from the darkness and pray. Hold the light of my predilection close to you: the Rosary. Pray it unceasingly. Pray, my children, and be prepared for the events that you are about to live through. My children, I wish for you only joy, but you must help me with your actions. I am calling you with love. Please respond with love.

Our Blessed Mother then gave the locutionist messages on the first four Commandments. (Messages on the rest of the Commandments came at later dates.)

FEBRUARY 25, 1992 — My dear child, many of my children are choosing Hell over eternal salvation. Pray ceaselessly for them. Please my heart in doing so and help me by your prayers. Many of my children fight to kill the unborn. They do not realize the severity of their actions. In the end, my child, I shall conquer and My Son's reign shall come upon the world, so entangled within the web of sin and darkness. Pray very much for all the souls who are on the road of perdition. My child, the time has arrived for the fulfillment of the events that I have foretold. Pray, so that my children will seek me and My Son and that they will return to the Father in Heaven. I am with you and I love each one of you, my children.

FEBRUARY 27, 1992 - (JESUS) — My dear child, I entreat you to write. Open your heart fully, My child. Open yourself to Me, to the graces of My mercy. Open your heart and with true repentance ask for My mercy. My child, you are only one, but I call many. They do not listen. Soon My mercy will come like a fire to purify their hearts, to purify all hearts. Do not doubt these words. The time has now arrived. Open your hearts and be ready to receive My overwhelming mercy. My dear child, do not fear, but pass this message on. Graces shall come from it, tempered with love and kindness. I love you and I am with you always. Pray ... My Mother has come to call you to this, to call mankind back to Me, your God.

FEBRUARY 28, 1992 — My dear child, tell everyone that I seek for them to come and pray before My Son, exposed in the monstrance. Come all of you, my children, and open your hearts before My Son, who is truly present in the Holy Eucharist. Do not doubt, rather have faith and pray. I love you all and I am with you.

FEBRUARY 28, 1992 - SECOND MESSAGE — My dear child, write for me ... know this, my children, beloved of my heart, that the purification is now at hand. Open your hearts and prepare for the flood of God's mercy. My children, afterward you will live in great times of sorrow. The favorable time of your return to God is soon coming to an end. Do not fear, though, my little ones, because I will be with you in your moments of extreme sorrow and distress. Do not forget, I, Your Mother, love you.

MARCH 4, 1992 — Do not fear because of those who doubt. Know that I am with you.

MARCH 5, 1992 — My dear children, again I call you to open your hearts with love and with sincerity. Please, do not mock My Son and me. I have chosen this parish and so I ask you to heed my call to conversion and peace. I am with you and I love you.

* This parish refers to Michael's home parish.

MARCH 5, 1992 - SECOND MESSAGE — My child, I call all of my children to sacrifice during Lent with love, to pray with love, to act with love. I am guiding you all to My Son, Whose return is soon to come.

MARCH 8, 1992 — My dear children, I desire this to be a place of prayer and reconciliation. My children, be reconciled! Go to Confession and pray very much. Pray to ease the sufferings of our hearts and for the conversion of sinners. Oh, my Immaculate Heart will triumph! Please, assist me and help me to defeat my adversary. I love you and I am with you.

* ... I desire this to be a place of prayer ... again refers to Michael's home parish.

MARCH 8, 1992 - SECOND MESSAGE - Message given for the Sunday Prayer Group — My dear child, please write ... I love you all my children, gathered here tonight to pray in union with me. My dear little ones, I am calling you now to pray <u>very</u> much. The times are serious. Please consecrate a time during your day to be with God and to pray. Pray especially for the unbelievers. I am very pleased with all of you. Continue to open your hearts and I will be able to continue to make of each one of you a blossoming flower for the Father. Thank you, my children.

MARCH 9, 1992 — My dear child, please write ... I am your loving and merciful Mother. I have come at this time to assist you and to call you to return to God and to open to My Son the doors of your hearts. I love you all, my little ones. Please, listen to my call. Pray very much everyday. Pray the Rosary with all your heart. Embrace the cross, that My Son has given you, with love. My children, live my messages with love. My children, again, I say to you all: open your hearts and return to My Son. I love you and I am with you. Prepare, my little ones, be ready, for you are now about to live through the great events of your time.

MARCH 12, 1992 — My dear children, I call you to pray very much. Your world is in great danger if you, my children, do not return to God and change your ways. My little ones, turn away from sin and open your hearts to the love of My Son and me. I am calling you with love. Please, my children, respond with love. Pray every day. Pray the Rosary and offer me your hearts. I love you and I am with you all, my children.

MARCH 12, 1992 - SECOND MESSAGE — My dear children, I love you all. This is why I have been with you for so long. I call you with the most serious urgency to respond to my wishes: to pray, fast, and do penance. My children, I will not be with you much longer. This is why you must open your hearts to receive the overflowing graces, as this is still the favorable time of God's mercy. My children, please listen to my call and respond.

MARCH 13, 1992 — My dear child, I call you to be open and attentive to my requests. Do not fear; I am with you. My children of Holy Name, I am with you. I am calling all of you and all of your brothers and sisters of this world to come back with open hearts to the ways of God; to return to My Son with love, to follow the Gospel teachings; to do so, my children, with love. I, Your Mother of All Mankind, am calling you to sincerely open your hearts; to pray: everyday the fifteen decade Rosary, to fast on bread and water, to do penance and make sacrifices for your sins. My children, I call you also to love one another and to open your hearts to Jesus so that you may be able to forgive and to live in peace. My children, I bless you and I leave you with the peace of My Son, Jesus. I love you all, my children, and I am with you.

MARCH 20, 1992 — My dear children, so beloved of my heart, you my children, I am calling with such love. Please, open your hearts with love and respond to me and my call with love and with sincerity. My children, I am sorrowful over the indifference to so many of my messages. Stop my tears, my children, with your action, with your prompt response to my call. Please, my dear little ones, begin by praying the Rosary from your heart everyday. Fast strictly at least one day a week. Go to Confession and do works of penance. Make sacrifices for your sins and for the sins and ingratitude of those in the world. My children, you do not have endless time to waste. Walk quickly out of the darkness you are in and come with love to me, your loving Mother. Return with love to My Son, Jesus Christ. Come, my children, return with love to your Father in Heaven, Who has sent me to call you all back to Him. My children, again, I say, respond with love. I love you all, my children, and I am with you. Go in God's peace.

MARCH 25, 1992 — My child, write ... I am the Woman Clothed with the Sun who has come in these times to lead mankind out of its great darkness and into the light of My Son. I have come to illuminate your paths and to fill you with the peace and joy of Heaven. My children, please pray the Rosary everyday. You receive many graces when you come to me and pray with your heart. I love you all, my children, and this is why I call you all now with great seriousness. You have begun the time of battle. My children, I call you all to decide for My Son in this battle and not for Satan and his temptations, which lure you away from the grace of My Son and into the den of sin. I love you. Please, my children, respond to my call with seriousness and with love from your heart. I am with you and I bless you all in the Name of the Father and the Son and the Holy Spirit. Go and live in the peace of God.

APRIL 1, 1992 — My dear children, gaze upon my image with love. I come to you as a loving and merciful Mother: a Mother who wishes to comfort you in your times of sorrow, a Mother who wishes to remedy your ills and your pains. My children, do not think that I do not hear you calling my name. Do not think, my children, that I do not see the tears you shed. My children, I come to you now with love and with an urgent message from Heaven. Look upon my Image of Our Lady of Guadalupe . See my loving gaze as I looked down upon Juan Diego, as I look now upon all of you. My children, pray the Rosary from your hearts. Pray with love and with sincerity. Come to me now ... ask for the mercy of my Son to come down upon each one of you. I love you all, my dear children. Come and look upon your Mother who comes to you with love, who comes to assuage and comfort, who comes in these darkened times to lead you all, by the hand, back to my Son, Our Lord and Savior, Jesus Christ. Celebrate the Mass with love and with repentance for your sins. Open your hearts to my Son, Who is present in the Eucharist and Who wishes to fill you with His light and thus transform each one of you into vessels of love, of light, and of mercy for the world. Go, my children, when you leave here tonight and spread my message and the light of my Son. I love you all and I, your Mother, am with you. Go, my children, in the peace of God.

APRIL 8, 1992 — My dear child, go and tell your pastor, my beloved son, Fr. O Connor, that I wish there to be exposition of the Most Blessed Sacrament at the Sunday night prayer group, beginning on the Feast of Divine Mercy, April 26. For I am the Mother of Divine Mercy and so I wish that all of my children come before my Son and open their hearts with love and with sincerity so that my Son may pour forth the mercy of His heart, which is aflame with love for mankind. Pray and make reparation before the Blessed Sacrament. I love you all and I am with you. Go in God's peace, . . please do not refuse my call. Thank you, my children, for your open hearts.

* When Michael began the Sunday night prayer group, he decided to give it the name Our Mother of Divine Mercy Rosary Prayer Group. It

could not have been foreseen that almost a year later Our Lady would ask for exposition of the Blessed Sacrament every Sunday night during the prayer group, starting on the Feast of Divine Mercy. Fr. O Connor graciously said "yes" to Our Lady's call.

APRIL 8, 1992 - SECOND MESSAGE — My dear children, listen closely to your Blessed Mother, who is calling you in these times to remain faithful to the Gospel, to remain faithful to my beloved Son, the Pope. Remain close to my Pope, who I have led and directed, who is consecrated to me.

Be strong and faithful in the storm, which as of now, you are living through, and which, in a greater way, you are about to live through. Remain close to the true teachings of the Catholic Church and veer away from those pastors and clergy who are not remaining faithful to Church teachings and who speak against my Pope.

My children, pray ... pray very much for the Pope and for those who will remain by his side in the times that are to come. Pray very much especially the Most Holy Rosary. Offer your prayers up for unity and faith, for the protection of the Pope and for fidelity to the Holy Father, who is carrying out the true teachings of the Roman Catholic Church. My children, remain close to me and you will remain close to the Holy Father.

My children, I leave you now with this message of urgency.

Pray and live with all your heart the messages, which from so many places throughout the world, I have been giving to this world, to a darkened and misguided humanity. I love you all and I am with you.

APRIL 10, 1992 — My dear child, please write for me. My children, the time of great mercy has come. Open your hearts to the Lord. My children, your time remaining is short ... the mercy is now being poured out over the world. The favorable time to return to God is now. My children, do not wait to see signs but listen and convert now. Return to the Lord, who has sent me to you in His infinite love and mercy. I have come once again to tell you all to pray, fast, and do penance. My children, pray, pray, pray very, very much. Do not waste this valuable time given to you by God. Use your time and open yourselves to the grace which the Father in Heaven wishes to pour forth. Open yourselves to the mercy of God. The time of justice is soon, my children. I love you all and I have come again to tell you with seriousness to return to the Lord. Go in God's peace.

APRIL 11, 1992 — My dear children of Holy Name, I have chosen my little soul so you may know that the hour of mercy has arrived. The Father in Heaven is calling all the world to return to Him. My children, with so much love for you, I call you to open yourselves to the grace and mercy of My Son, who has sent me to give you messages. My children, I come to call you to pray, to fast, to repent of your sins, and to return to the ways of God. Convert your lives and sin no more. Turn away from all sin and open yourselves to the love of God so that He may make of you, with His love and mercy, beautiful, pure, blossoming souls. Open yourselves to the mercy of Jesus. My children, I call you with love; please respond with love and with sincerity. My children, I love you and I am with you. Go in God's peace.

APRIL 16, 1992 - HOLY THURSDAY — My dear children, this night you celebrate the institution of the Holy Eucharist. As My Son eats His Last Supper with the apostles He also prepares for the coming events, His Passion to come and His death. My children, you too are now on the verge of the great events of your time. My children, partake of this Eucharistic celebration with love in your hearts. Be prepared for what is to come, my children, the passion of your time. My children, behold, My Son, who leaves with you for all time His presence in the Holy Eucharist. My children, rejoice and be thankful.

APRIL 17, 1992 - GOOD FRIDAY — My children, today I come to you as the Mother of Great Sorrow. Today Simeon's prophecy is fulfilled. The sword of sorrow pierces my heart. Behold, my children, My Son, Jesus, who hangs on the Cross in redemption for the sins of the world. Look upon the uncountable number of wounds and lacerations which cover His body from the scourging at the pillar; the crown of thorns upon His sacred head; the nails which pierce His hands and feet, and the wound in His side. My children, the blood, which My Son shed for humanity, covers His wounded body. My children, meditate on the Passion of Jesus. Look upon my face and see the tears I shed continuously. Unite your prayers with my great sorrow. Open your hearts and behold ... the Son of Man, who came to take away the sins of the world.

Behold, Jesus nailed to the cross. I leave you now my children. Go and pray before the Cross.

APRIL 19, 1992 - EASTER SUNDAY — My dear children, rejoice and be glad! The Son of Man, Who came to take away the sins of the world, Who died on the Cross for all of you, has risen from the dead. My children, rejoice and let your hearts be filled with joy. The Son of Man has conquered sin and death. On this day, my children, I call you to open your hearts and to look upon the risen Jesus. The tears that now fall from my eyes are tears of joy. My children, unite yourselves and let joy and peace fill your hearts. This is the day the Lord has made. Rejoice, my children, and be glad.

APRIL 21, 1992 - (JESUS) — During my prayer of the Sorrowful Mysteries of the Holy Rosary, I received an interior vision of Our Lord's face profile with His head slightly bowed and the crown of thorns weaved into His head causing a strong flow of blood into Jesus' face. He then spoke these words to me:

Offer My Holy Face to the Father in atonement for the sins of all mankind.

APRIL 26, 1992 - (JESUS) - FEAST OF DIVINE MERCY — My dear child, today is the day of My great mercy. Today, My mercy is poured out upon all humanity. My children, come to Me and ask for forgiveness for all of your sins. Come and wash in My mercy and My love. Come to the fount of My mercy and cleanse yourselves of sin. Today, My children, I come to you as the Merciful Savior.

MAY 3, 1992 — My dear children, I come in these days as the Woman Clothed With The Sun, as the Queen of Heaven. I come to lead all of my children away from the darkness of the world and to the light of my Son, Jesus Christ. I call you all to turn to me and to heed the warning with which I come down from Heaven. My children, consecrate yourselves to me so that I may better lead you along the paths of penance and prayer. My children, I tell you, the days of mercy and grace are no longer in such abundance; therefore I call you seriously to listen closely to the messages I bring and to live them with all your heart.

My children, respond quickly and with seriousness. Make the decision to turn from sin and toward the Father in Heaven. My children, turn away from the darkness and come to the light. Come, my children. I love you all, my little ones, and I am with you. Come close to my heart and entrust yourselves to me. I am your sure guide to Jesus.

MAY 9, 1992 — My dear children, I am urgently calling you all to respond to the messages that I have come with. My children, do you not realize the times you live in? You continue to try and make your way in the great darkness of the world. My children, open your hearts to my messages. Open your hearts to My Son and let Him enter. My children, Jesus calls each one of you to be pure and humble and to follow Him by taking up your crosses day after day and following Him with love in your hearts. My children, I love you all and this is why I tell you with seriousness that you do not have much time before the justice of God falls on the world. My children, you are being called to the light. Why do you not respond? Those of you who have listened to my call, I ask you to pray with even more fervor and to fast with serious intention for the unbelievers. My children, all of you, whom I love so much, I call you to pray the Rosary daily and to make frequent visits to My Son, present in the tabernacles of your churches. Come and comfort the heart of My Son with your prayers and with your love. My children, I love you all and I am with you. Please, open your hearts so that I may guide you along the path of salvation and lead you all to My Son, Jesus Christ. My children, please respond to my call of urgency and of love. I bless you all in the Name of the Father, and the Son, and the Holy Spirit.

MAY 9, 1992 - SECOND MESSAGE — My dear children, of Holy Name, I send you my little soul to call you to the messages which I have given to him for all of you, for all of mankind. I am your Mother and as a Mother I have watched over all of you. I have watched you stray from My Son and from me. I have watched you get caught and lost in the depths of sin. I have taken care of you and have watched over you at every moment and I have come to call you all in a special way back to my Son, Our Lord and Savior, Jesus Christ. I call upon each one of you to listen and respond to the messages which I bring from Heaven. I call you to pray, especially the Most Holy Rosary. I call you to go to Confession frequently. I call you to do penance and fast. My children, my messages to you are serious. I ask you all to open your hearts and to respond with love to what I have asked of you. The Father in Heaven has given each of you the free will to accept or reject the messages which I have given and which I continue to give. But I ask you with the loving and merciful heart of a Mother to listen to me and to respond to my call. My children, do not forget that I am with you and that I love you all. My children, go in God's peace.

MAY 23, 1992 — My dear children, so beloved of my heart, I ask you in these days that you remain close to my maternal heart so that I may protect you. My children, in a serious way I call you to pray the Rosary and to make fasting a serious priority in these days. My children, please use this time of grace, that God has given you, to its fullest. My children, your time of mercy is short and so I tell you with great urgency to pray, fast, and make reparation for your sins. Those of you who are far from my heart and my Son's heart, I call you with love to return to the Father, to return to my Son, Who awaits you not with anger and justice but with love and mercy. My children, listen closely to my words and live them with your heart. Do not just go through the actions of what I have asked of you, but live these messages with your hearts. Live the messages with love.

Thank you, my children. I love you all and I am with you. Please pray, ... pray, my children, very much.

MAY 24, 1992 — My children, the time of your great trial has almost come. The time when my adversary will be enthroned in the hearts of men and those who follow my Son will be laughed at. They will be greatly persecuted. You, my children, are the little flock who I am leading and guiding at every step along your arduous journey. You must know that the times ahead will be rough for all the world. My children, I call you at this time to continuous prayer and sacrifices.

My children, you are now about to begin the most horrible of times. Prepare by consecrating yourselves to my heart and to the heart of my Son. Prepare by living the messages and by seeking the mercy of my Son. I am with you, my children, and I will not abandon you in the days ahead.

OPEN YOUR HEARTS

JUNE 4, 1992 — My dear child, so beloved of my heart, I come to you on this day of rest for you. I am very pleased with your father and with you and with the work of my dear little daughter. My children, I come to ask you again to continue to pray for the unbelievers and to continue to grow in the love of my Son. I love you and I am with you.

JUNE 10, 1992 — My dear child, please write for me. My heart is sorrowful over the decision of so many of my children to turn away from God and from the graces that He is bestowing upon humanity at this time.

Oh, my children, do you not realize the great importance of opening your hearts to the great gift that God is giving you in allowing me to come to all of you? My children, my adversary is sowing confusion and uncertainty into your hearts and is slowly and insidiously leading you to commit acts of sin against God. He is leading you and your families away from God by causing problems and disruptions within your families and within your lives. My children, you are so precious to me and this is why I continue to call you to repentance and to prayer. This is why I call you to look upon my words and to live them with your hearts so that you may be transformed and renewed by love. This is why I tirelessly continue to assist you through these messages, to help you understand the great importance of placing God at the center of your lives. My children, listen closely to the messages I bring. Open your hearts, my dear little ones. Consecrate yourselves and your families to my Immaculate Heart so that I may protect you from Satan and his subtle snares with which he tries to ruin your lives.

My children, please be open at every moment to the grace of God. My children, listen now and listen with seriousness.

I love you all and I am with you. Do not doubt my motherly presence among you. I am keeping watch over all of you. My children, go in God's peace and live with love these messages.

JUNE 19, 1992 — My children, so beloved of my heart, I tell you today that I love you. I tell you all that I am with you and am continually guiding you. I am your loving and merciful Mother.

My children, today I call you again to repentance and to prayer. I call you all to go to Confession and to cleanse yourselves of all sin. I call you also to pray. Pray especially the Rosary, which I love so much.

Offer me each Our Father and Hail Mary as a beautiful budding rose. My children, in this way, too, become budding flowers that I can present to the Father in Heaven. My children, you are all mine and this is why I tell you continually to make an act of consecration to my Immaculate Heart and to my Son's Sacred Heart so that we may protect you and fill you with the love of Heaven. My children, I call you to live peace and to live love.

I call you in these days of unrest to forgive one another.

My children, reconcile yourselves with God through Confession and through prayer. My children, be reconciled, also, with one another. Come to the heart which overflows with mercy and love, ... the heart of my Son. Come and cleanse yourselves in this heart. Come, my children, and drink of my Son's mercy and love. My children, come to the Fount of Mercy, the Sacred Heart of Jesus. My children, I love you all, and so, I do not tire in telling you again that I desire you to pray and to love. Go in God's peace, my children.

JULY 23, 1992 — My dear child, continue to pray with all your heart so that my Son and I may work the miracle of God's grace and love within your life.

My children, you have entered into the decisive times of battle. You live now, my children, within the time of trial and so I ask you to continue to pray with open and sincere hearts and to listen and live the message I bring.

I love you and I am with you.

AUGUST 1, 1992 — My children, how I have come to every part of the earth to give you messages asking you to return to the ways of God! Even in tears do I come to help you realize the great importance of my messages. But so many of you have not listened.

Sin continues to spread across the world. The grave sin of abortion continues to be practiced, thus causing my motherly heart great pain at seeing the slaughter of millions of unborn children.

My children, I continue to repeat again and again to you the way of salvation and the way of peace, the way of putting God in the center of your lives. First, my children, you must begin to decide for God in all things. Put God first in your lives and all else will blossom. Secondly, you must pray so that you can cultivate the seeds of faith and love. My children, I call you to pray every day, especially the Holy Rosary. With the Rosary you can destroy all the darkness which surrounds you. With the Rosary, you can bring peace into your lives and work the grace of God's love and mercy into the lives of others.

My children, I call you also to fast and do penance. Fasting is so important, my children, and so pertinent to your conversion. I call you to go to Confession frequently to wash away all of your sins, to cleanse yourselves of all sin. My children, make use of this great sacrament. So many of you have turned away from this sacrament and thus you have let sin cover you and fill you with darkness and with an apathy for repentance. This has further darkened your understanding and love of Mass and of your reception of the Eucharist in a state of grace at Holy Communion. My children, please go to Confession.

My children, I leave you now with another message. I ask you to listen and to realize what I am saying to you and to realize also the importance of this message. I will not be with you like this always. Realize, my little children, this grace. Realize this great gift from God. I love you all, my precious little ones, and I am with you.

AUGUST 9, 1992 — My child, the year 1993 is slowly approaching. In this year the storm of God's justice will grow and its effects will be seen in a greater way throughout the entire world. Your time of conversion is short and so I tell you now to pray without ceasing.

My children, oh my precious ones, why have you not listened to me? Now, in a very serious way, I tell you to be open to my Son's mercy. Love one another and seek forgiveness.

My children, work towards peace, because your days, filled with sin, are continuing to destroy peace. Again, I tell you with motherly love ... I love you and I am with you.

AUGUST 18, 1992 — My child, the nation which lies hidden in the eyes of the world will be the cause of much destruction. I come again to call you to pray for my intentions so that many more of my children may consecrate themselves to my Immaculate Heart and so that Satan's plans may be defeated. In this way you will bring peace into the world and a greater number of souls will be saved.

* In an interview with Michael Brown (author of *The Final Hour, Witness: Josyp Terelya Apparitions in the USSR* and *Prayer of The War-*

rior) Michael McColgan spoke about the messages which he was receiving and in particular about this message. McColgan shared with Brown who the nation was and Brown agreed, sharing with McColgan that other visionaries that he had interviewed and in whom he had faith had told him the same thing. (This reference to Mr. Brown is not meant to say that Michael Brown has, in his opinion, approved of the revelations to Michael). It is important that the reader not worry about the country but focus on the essence of the messages, which is the need to pray for all countries and for all peoples.

AUGUST 31, 1992 — My children, the world is immersed in such a great darkness and daily countless numbers of souls are being lost. My children, I ask you once again today to look upon the messages which I am bringing and to realize their great importance. You continue to be lukewarm in your response and this has caused many of your brothers and sisters to be lost in sin, instead of being saved by your belief and by your actions within their lives. My children, I continue to cry tears, even of blood, and I continue to come to you telling you of the great danger you are in, but so many of you act as if none of this mattered. My children, the hours of suffering which lie ahead of you are so awful that you cannot even imagine how bad it will be for this world. This is why I come day after day to remind you of the importance of refusing to live in sin. My children, open your hearts and decide for God. Please, my little ones, listen now while the mercy of my Son is at your door, for I tell you with great seriousness that the hour of my Son's justice has now arrived. Do not wait for it to come upon the earth in all its power, but listen now. Repent of your sins, cleanse yourselves and return to my Son. My children, listen to me, hear my words, respond with love and live them with seriousness. I love you all and I am with you.

SEPTEMBER 5, 1992 — My dear children, today I come to ask you to offer one sacrifice up to me, with love, for all of my intentions. Your days of mercy are great but they are numbered and so I call you to be open in a greater way to what God desires of each of you. My children, I ask also, again, that you pray the Rosary with love. When you take time out of your day to pray, hold some time in silence, and speak with God from your heart.

My children, this moment of silence should be used to tell God that you love Him, to thank Him for His innumerable gifts to you, and also to ask pardon for your sins. My children, be open to the messages which I am bringing to you. Listen and realize what I am asking of you. My children, I tell you with seriousness, ... live the messages, so that you may find peace, ... peace which can only come through a closer and more intimate union with God. I love you and I am with you.

SEPTEMBER 21, 1992 — My dear children, the great trial for humanity continues to intensify as your days of mercy continue to become shorter in number. I ask you again, my children, to pray the Rosary with all of your heart. I call you again today to live with seriousness the messages which I have brought from Heaven. My children, the signs of God's justice will soon become more and more apparent. Pray, my children. Do not cease in praying and making reparation in atonement for the sins and grave injustices of mankind. Oh, my little ones, the days ahead of you will be terrible unless you listen to me and use this time of great grace and mercy.

Pray, my children, and seek first in these days the Kingdom of God.

SEPTEMBER 23, 1992 — My children, today again, I come to warn you of the great danger you are in. You have not, in a great way, listened to my serious call. You have not, as I had wished, listened to and responded to my call. Oh, my little ones, so beloved of my heart, I desire you to know that I love you so very much. I shall continue to come to you to assist you on the path which my Son has, through the Gospel teachings, made for you. But I tell you also that I need you to take with seriousness the call with which I now come. This year, 1992, has been a year of trouble for your world. It has been marked by decisive events which are preparing for all that which is now about to come upon you. This is why I ask you with the love and with the care and worry of a Mother to pray and to fast, and to repent of your sins. My children, simply, I tell you to return to God and the ways which in His great love and mercy, He has set for you. My children, call upon my Son for mercy. Listen now, my children. Do not wait.

SEPTEMBER 25, 1992 — My dear children, so beloved of my heart, I come again today to bring the light of my Son, Jesus. I come again to ask you to pray the Rosary and to fast. My children, please listen to my words. Heed my requests and my warnings. My Son desires to pour forth upon this darkened world innumerable amounts of grace and mercy. My children, this is the time of Divine Mercy. I come to bring you this light and mercy so that your lives may be transformed in the peace and love of God. My children, your world is continuing to drift into darkness. I call you, therefore, to listen and to respond with love and with sincerity as I have asked again and again. My children, I do not wish to continue to admonish you. I have already informed you, through my messages to you here, through my little chosen soul, and through my words to you throughout the world, of the imminent danger that you are in. My children, I tell you again and again of the trial which you are now living through, but to no avail. Many of you continue to act as if the messages I bring are of no worth or are only fantasy in the eyes of many of my children, who are listening to my requests. My Son is preparing justice for the world. I come to you to ask you to repent and to change your ways. My children, what you sow is what you shall reap. Turn away from my adversary, who sows lies, dissension, confusion, hatred, lust and greed into the hearts of so many. I call you to look to the light, to be open to the light, which is my Son, Jesus Christ. My children, I come to prepare this errant world for the splendor and glory of the new times which are now at your doorstep. But before this can come, the world must be purified and Satan must be defeated. My Immaculate Heart shall triumph and the Eucharistic Heart of Jesus will reign supreme in the hearts of all men. Jesus is the King of Kings and the Lord of Lords. He is the Prince of Peace. As of now the world and all of humanity prepares for the prince of darkness to come and reign upon his throne for the time which has been given to him.

Peace, my children, is unattainable if you do not gain it through your return to God and through His Laws of Love. My children, I, your Mother, come today to tell you to look to Heaven, ... to realize the blatant signs of your times: my numerous appearances throughout the world, the uprising of wars, the continuing natural disasters. My children, this will continue in a greater and far worse way if humanity does not accept my plea for conversion. The hearts of men lie hidden and bare. They cry out for love amidst a diseased world. Oh, my children, please listen to my call. Please respond. Pray the Rosary. Go to Confession asking the Lord for pardon of your sins. Walk along the path of conversion. Follow and live the Gospel teachings of Jesus. Oh, my children, realize the great and urgent importance of my call. I leave you now in God's peace. Go and live the messages. Again, I tell you, open your hearts to the Lord.

SEPTEMBER 25, 1992 - SECOND MESSAGE — My children, I exhort you to pray every day the Most Holy Chaplet of Divine Mercy to bring down upon you the great mercy of my Son.

OCTOBER 11, 1992 — My child, I am very pleased with you. (Pause) Prepare for the calamities. Pray **VERY** much.

OCTOBER 13, 1992 — My child, today again I come to you as the Mother of All Mankind. I come on this, the 75th anniversary of my last apparition in Fatima to my three little angels, ... Francisco and Jacinta, who are now both in Heaven with me and also Lucia, who continues to be with you. My children, I have spoken to you again and again of your times and of the great danger that humanity is in. This is the last hour. My children, I tell you, the world will tremble and the justice of God will be seen. Prepare for this with unceasing prayer and with acts of mortification and reparation. My children, I come to you today also as the Queen of All Hearts and as the Lady of the Holy Rosary. I come to you with my arms outstretched and in one hand my weapon given to you for your protection and as a refuge of sanctity to help you along your path of conversion. Oh, my little ones, so beloved of my Immaculate Heart! Today I ask again for the recitation of the fifteen decades of the Holy Rosary. I come to ask also, that you stop offending God, who is greatly offended. My children, I tell you again, the cup of justice is flowing over. The purification of the world must come. My children, the hour has now arrived. Pray! Stay awake and keep watch. I am with you always, my little ones.

OCTOBER 16, 1992 — My children, on this the Feast of St. Margaret Mary Alacoque, I desire to tell you of my Son's great love for mankind. I desire to tell you of my Son's unfathomable mercy and of the light and love which flows from His Sacred Heart. My children, open your little hearts to my Son and to His never-ending mercy. My children, this is the time of conversion. Be reconciled quickly. Do not turn away from this grace. I am with you, my children, to remind you constantly of the love and mercy of my Son. My children, come drink at the fountain of mercy. Come one and all to the Sacred Heart of Jesus, which burns with desire to love the world. My children, pray and make reparation for mankind's great sin, that of offending the heart of my Son. My children, repent and return to the one triune God. I love you all, my little ones. You are all precious to me.

NOVEMBER 16, 1992 — My dear child, this message I wish you to give to your bishop. Tell him that it is my wish that he call upon the pastors of your diocese to have a vigil on the eve of the Feast of the Immaculate Conception. I wish that my Son be exposed upon the altar and that the people of each parish come before my Son to ask for mercy and pardon for the great sin of your country and of the world.

The people should be instructed to pray all 15 decades of the Rosary: the Joyful, Sorrowful, and Glorious Mysteries. Also, I wish that at the end of this prayer they call upon my Son in a greater way through the prayer of the Chaplet of Divine Mercy. On this feast day my motherly presence will enshroud you and my mantle of peace will cover all the diocese. My Son will bless all the pastors who are vigilant in doing His work. Let them call upon their flock to open their hearts to my Son and to me, who am the Mother of All. My child, tell the bishop that this is my desire. May you all be open to the mercy of my Son, Our Lord and Savior, Jesus Christ. I am with you.

* Concerning this message: You are invited to do this in your own Church in your Diocese, each year, at this time.

NOVEMBER 16, 1992 - SECOND MESSAGE — My dear child, please write for me.

I have not come to you in some time because I have desired to strengthen you through this cross. Know, my child, that humanity is, as of now, at the edge of the precipice. Humanity has continued to walk down the dark road of sin and so justice is now about to come to purify the earth and its inhabitants.

My child, know that I have come for so long to urge you all to repentance, but so many have refused my call.

Many also, have heard, believed, and then turned away, led once again down the path of unrighteousness. Call upon my Son. Call upon His mercy, which is never-ending.

Pray and make many sacrifices for what is about to unfold. My child, pray for the bishop and for the priests within your diocese that they accept my call to return to my Son in a strong way once again. Many of my priest-sons ignore my call and so they have turned away from the grace prepared for them and for their flock. I am with him (the bishop) and am protecting him from various dangers. Pray for the Pope, my children. You, my priest-sons, consecrate yourselves to me in a greater way so that I may strengthen you in carrying your crosses and may in a greater way perfect your priesthood. I am your Mother. I am the Mother of All.

Come to me and seek shelter from the storm. I will give you protection and I will lead you all back to my Son. The Church shall be renewed, as will all humanity. Pray, for the hour has come. Seek forgiveness. Wait and watch. Trust in my words to you.

NOVEMBER 16, 1992 - THIRD MESSAGE — My child, write ... pray ceaselessly for the souls who are, as of now, on the road of perdition. Pray for the Holy Father and for all priests because their cross will become great. Offer many, many sacrifices for the priests and all religious. My children, what must God do to awaken you? You have scoffed at the apparitions and my motherly words to you, but you will not scoff at the justice of God, who is now about to lay forth His hand upon the earth for its wickedness.

It is now, the moment has arrived. Pray without ceasing and no longer offend God. Pray, pray, pray, and stop my tears of sorrow. I love you all and I am with you, my children. Realize, with importance, the hour you are in and the hour through which you must live. Pray for the grace of God to fill your homes and your hearts. Be at peace and hope in the Lord.

NOVEMBER 17, 1992 — The moment has come. Pray very much and offer up many sacrifices. I wish for you to be my little soul of reparation.

DECEMBER 4, 1992 — My dear child, the time has come for my Son to let down upon the world His hand of justice. This is why, in so many apparitions, my messages have become more urgent. Again, I call you all to prayer: a prayer full of love and from the heart. It is not enough just to say the prayers. You must mean them. When you begin to pray from your heart with love you will then understand, truly, why I have come to you. My children, know that your country will suffer. Great trials are ahead of you and for all humanity. Many have not listened to my warnings. They have not repented of their sins, but have continued to offend God, ... some even in greater ways. My children, the time of the great purification is upon you. For this reason, I again call you all to vigilant prayer and fasting. Pray with all of your hearts and seek forgiveness from God for your sins. My children, listen closely to what I tell you and please live the messages. It is for your own good, for the good of your souls, of your families, and for the world. Pray, pray, pray and seek forgiveness. I love you all and I leave with you the peace of my Son. Go in peace, my children.

DECEMBER 4, 1992 - SECOND MESSAGE — My child, add this prayer, and ask people to recite it many times and to pray it with deep sincerity before the Cross. My children, ask my Son for mercy and pray for your country.

My Lord and my God, have mercy on me. I am a poor, miserable sinner. I have offended You greatly with my sins, but now I come to You seeking forgiveness, seeking Your mercy, seeking to be loved and to love. Jesus, my Savior, merciful Lord, Your mercy is endless I ask You now to have mercy on me, to cleanse me of my darkness and to fill my heart and mind with Your light. My Jesus, my God, have mercy on me. I am Your child, faithful, now and forever. Amen.

DECEMBER 21, 1992 — Dear children, in these days I desire that you look to those around you and try to see good in everyone even those who do not show it. I call you to peace and to show the light of my Son, to spread the light of my Son. For this you must be open to all that my Son desires to do within your hearts. Be open to love. Forgive one another. Be a light, my children, in the ever-increasing darkness of the world. Pray and be reconciled in this season of joy.

DECEMBER 22, 1992 — Dear children, for so long I have called you to interior recollection. I have called you to bring the messages into your hearts — to take them there and to meditate on my words to you.

Why this? Because I desire that you fully understand and comprehend not just with your minds, but also, and more importantly, with your hearts. My children, I am with you and I love you with a sincere love — the love of a Mother. I desire that you fully understand this ... that I am with you. I wish for you to live the message that I give. My children, at this moment in history it is especially important for you to live the messages so that you may help me to defeat the plans of my adversary and also for your conversion and salvation. My children, sincerely I tell you, live the messages; live them with sincerity and with love. This means, my children, to want to live them; to look forward each day to your time with God; to desire to do penance and to fast. My children, pray with your whole heart — pray and feel each word. Live your actions of prayer. This means, my children, that when you stop your prayer of words begin your prayer of actions: good deeds, charity toward others, forgiveness when others harm you by words or actions, and especially by loving all those around you, regardless.

My children, as this important and eventful year closes, I wish to leave you with this word: love. Meditate on God's great love for all of you. Meditate on my Son's constant love for all of you. My children, realize also my undying love for all of you. Pray, my little ones, that the Holy Spirit may descend upon you so that you may have the strength to carry your cross in this coming year. Pray, my children, and may your living of the messages be a constant joy for you. I leave you now with the peace of my Son. Go and evangelize. Tell the world of God and of the light with which my Son desires to fill hearts. Go, my children, and love.

DECEMBER 22, 1992 - SECOND MESSAGE — My children, realize the great importance of my messages. So many in the world are clothed in sin and their hearts are filled with darkness. My children, pray and make many sacrifices. This year, that is about to come, will be a year of great temptation. Pray only and seek the will of God, daily, in your lives. Realize with urgency what I have come to ask for. Pray and make sacrifices and place God and His will first in your lives, my children.

DECEMBER 22, 1992 - THIRD MESSAGE — My children, listen very closely to my words of these past few days. Pray with sincerity and be open to all that God desires to do with you and within your hearts. My children, when I say to you that this year to come will be one of temptation, I mean that many will be tempted to question their faith in little ways. Many will be tempted to turn away from God through actions and words unbecoming a believer. Many will be led further down the perverse road of lust and impurity. My children, I have called you in this year to be open to God and to live the messages that I have brought to you in a stronger way so that you may be prepared for the trials which await you. My children, pray and fast. Turn away from the ways of the world — the ways of selfishness, of pride, of lust and impurity, of sin. Do not continue to be weak in your faith and in your actions. Believe and live in a serious way the Commandments of God. Place God first in your hearts and lives. In this way, my children, you will comprehend the meaning of my coming and the seriousness of your times.

DECEMBER 25, 1992 - CHRISTMAS DAY — Dear children, today I come to you as the Mother of Joy. I come today to call you to love and to be open to God and all that He desires to give to you. Especially, my children, with love, carry your crosses so that you may grow on your path of conversion and holiness. My children, pray to be able to do the will of God in your everyday life. My children, with joy I announce to you the birth of Jesus — the birth of the Light of the World. Pray, my children, seek God's will, seek the light. Seek my Son in your everyday lives.

My children, be joyful and be at peace on this joyous occasion. My Son, the Light of the World, has been born. The great night is broken by the ever increasing light which began with the birth of Jesus, which you celebrate on this day. Go in the Holy Child's peace. Go, my children, and live in peace. I love you all and I am with you!

OPEN YOUR HEARTS

OPEN YOUR HEARTS

MESSAGES FROM THE YEAR 1993

JANUARY 16, 1993 — My children, I ask you to pay serious attention to this message. Your country and the world, as a whole, are in great danger if mankind continues to go along the path of sin and darkness and does not heed my request of conversion, prayer, penance, and an overall return to God and a renewal of love for one's neighbor and for the Father in Heaven, Who desires your conversion with such love. My children, I can no longer hold back the hand of my Son. The time of grace and conversion is almost at its end; the time of justice has come. There is still time my children. Open your hearts and listen to my motherly plea. Listen to my call of conversion. My little ones, if you only knew what awaits you, you would not spare even one moment in embracing your God and His love. My children, there can be no turning back unless you return to God.

The purification will come. Pray to lessen its severity and to save souls. Pray my little ones. Seek God first. Come and partake of the Sacrament of Reconciliation and of the Eucharist, in which my Son, Jesus, is **TRULY** present. My children, listen closely to my warning. You are on the verge of the greatest events that the world has ever seen. The time of triumph has begun. Satan's defeat is sure. Pray and seek only the Kingdom of God. I desire all of my children to be saved.

JANUARY 17, 1993 (JESUS) — Let them know the urgency of My request through My Mother.

JANUARY 21, 1993 (JESUS) — Write for Me, My child. Come to Me, all of you who are tired and covered in sin and in the darkness which sin brings into your hearts. Come and seek mercy, My people. I await your full return. Open your hearts to Me, Your Lord. My people, listen well to the messages that My Mother now brings to you. They are the precursor of My justice. Mercy is now; the time of return, My people, is now. Open your hearts and receive My love in full abundance. Come to My heart and seek forgiveness for your numerous sins. My people, respond while there is still time. I come now with mercy, but if you refuse this, then My justice will come to cleanse the earth. I am a God of mercy and justice. You can decide which you want. My people, come to Me, Your ever-loving and merciful Lord.

JANUARY 21, 1993 — My little one, your Mother comes to you now with a serious message for those who will listen. The hour is close. Pray now without ceasing. You are on the brink of all that I have forewarned. My Son is not amused with the actions of the world toward its God. He is gravely hurt by the numerous sins and sacrileges committed against Him and against His Holy Mother.

My children, repent and throw yourselves down before His mercy. My children, pray the Rosary every day and ease the pains suffered by my heart because of the great injustice of mankind. Oh, my children, you will lament greatly for your slow and lack response to my urgent call. Pray, pray, pray.

JANUARY 25, 1993 — My children, I call you to pray and to place God first in your lives so that you will not put the ways of the world before the ways of God.

Pray and be reconciled.

JANUARY 27, 1993 — My child, pray very much. My Son and I will guide you so that you will know the right time for everything. Pray unceasingly because the devil is about to begin his onslaught upon the chosen souls. Pray also, so that you may continue to find God's favor and to rest in His peace.

Pray, my children. Pray without ceasing. May God's peace be with you.

FEBRUARY 2, 1993 — My dear little ones, it is important for you to focus on why I have come to you. It is to lead you to God, to lead you to my Son, Savior and Lord, Jesus Christ. My children, I come to lead you down a new path - the path that leads to Paradise. You will not attain this end if you follow the way of the world and the path that it has made, upon which so many souls now walk. Pray, my children, so that your hearts may be open to God and all that He desires to do within your lives. Do His most perfect will. Be open, my little ones, to God, the Father, Who desires your conversion. He has sent me to you so that you may know the truth and not be blinded by Satan and his tricks.

My children, look upon me, the Gentle Woman, your Mother. I come to lead you all back to God, ... to peace, to joy ... which you will obtain by placing God at the center of your lives. For this end, pray, fast and convert. Do not wait, my children. The time is now. The grace of God be with you all.

FEBRUARY 3, 1993 — My dear little ones, you beloved of my maternal heart. Today I come to you seeking prayers for the Pope, all bishops and priests, and also all those in religious life. My children, their cross in these days of darkness is great. And so, I come asking for sacrifices and prayers from you for them. My children, pray very much for the Church, ... Calvary is ahead. Pray, pray, pray.

My children, work hard to attain Paradise. My children, pray and realize the greatness of my calling you in these days. I am with you, little children.

FEBRUARY 3, 1993 - SECOND MESSAGE — *Michael had an overwhelming feeling of sorrow come over him during this message, as if he could feel the sorrow of the Blessed Mother. Michael said that this had not occurred before.

Michael, Michael, ... Michael, my child. Oh, ... pray very much for the Pope, who at this hour is in great danger. Offer your life, in a spirit of sacrifice and prayer for him. The darkness will become great at his departure. Pray only and keep silence with me. I wish to guide you down a deeper path of holiness. Open your heart and mortify yourself to God's will. Offer up every worry and be at peace, for my Son and I are with you all.

FEBRUARY 13, 1993 — Realize, my children, the importance of your times. Pray without ceasing so that you may find joy and live your days in peace with God. I love you and I am with you all.

FEBRUARY 14, 1993 — My child, write for me. Oh, my children, you are so close to my heart. I love you all and daily I pray for your peace and for your salvation.

Daily I come down from Heaven to give you messages so that you may know my love, as your Mother; so that you may begin anew each day to open your hearts to my Son and to me, your Mother. Oh, my children, so beloved of my heart, why do you not listen to my motherly plea? Why do my messages of conversion and repentance fall on so many deaf ears? My children, I do not come to joke with you, but I come with a very serious message: a message that the Father in Heaven has sent me to give to you. Convert, while there is still time. Repent of your sins; go to Confession. Follow the Commandments to the letter; do not pick and choose what you will believe, ... but follow and live with your whole heart the Commandments ... fully.

Live the law of God, ... live in His most perfect will by being open to the inspiration of the Holy Spirit. Pray the Rosary daily and live in peace and in humble silence. I am your Mother, my children, and I am always at your side. When there is any difficulty, do not hesitate to call on me.

I will be there for you. I have come to guide you all and to lead you to my Son. My children, please understand this and begin to live the messages more fully and with your hearts. Realize their great importance.

This is not a time to joke but it is a time to be serious and to follow the Lord with love and with sincerity.

Whoever is not with my Son is against Him. My children, choose to follow my Son and in this way you will choose salvation for your souls. Go in the peace of God, my little ones, and know that I am always at your side. I love you all.

FEBRUARY 14, 1993 - SECOND MESSAGE — My child, the Church of my Son will be shaken unto its very foundations. Satan will believe he has triumphed in the hour to come, but my Son will show him that this is not his victory ... that it is only an empty promise made to those unto his kingdom ... upon which it is built, ... lies. My children, seek only the will of God and unite yourselves more perfectly with my Son in the sacrifice of the Mass. My children, the hour has come. Pray, pray, pray ... and seek God's most perfect will.

FEBRUARY 15, 1993 - MESSAGE ON THE CHAPLET OF TRUTH — Oh my child, please write ... My children, the hour is close and the purification is now at hand, pray ... please, my children.

The Church faces its greatest hour of apostasy and so I ask you to take hold of your Rosaries and pray this chaplet. It will be called the Chaplet of Truth, because the Church which my Son began before He ascended into Heaven is the one, true Church-infallible, universal.

My children, you will begin by praying from your hearts the Apostles' Creed and then one Our Father. The Apostles' Creed, because it holds within it the truths for the faithful upon which the Church is built. The Our Father, because it is the prayer that my Son taught to you while He was upon the earth. Then you will pray three Hail Marys — one for the Church Triumphant, one for the Church Militant, and one for the Church Suffering. I am Mother and Queen of the Church; invoke me through the Hail Marys.

Then you will pray one Glory Be for the greater glory of the Most Holy Trinity.

My child, upon the beads of the Rosary you will pray, on the Our Father Beads - **"Father in Heaven, protect the true and infallible Church of which Your Son is Lord and King. Protect the faithful and strengthen and fill with grace Your servants within the Church, the priests and religious. Father in Heaven, give wisdom in grace to the Holy Father and to the bishops. Protect and guide, always, Your Church Militant, Suffering, Triumphant..."** and upon the Hail Mary beads **"Father, Son, and Holy Spirit, Triune God, pour out upon the Church divine grace, so that it may continue to unify the faithful and teach upon the earth the words of Our Lord and Savior, Jesus Christ, Redeemer of Mankind."**

My children, faithfully pray this chaplet with the words I have given you. Pray with your hearts. Pray, my children. At the end of this chaplet I desire that you again pray three Hail Marys, one Hail Holy Queen, and one Glory Be.

The three Hail Marys, to again call upon me, your Mother and Mother of the Church, for the protection of the truth, held within the teachings of the Church, ... the Hail Holy Queen, to invoke me as your Queen, and the Glory Be, to again, within your hearts and minds, offer to the Most Holy Trinity love and respect.

Pray for the Church. Speak in favor of your Church. When people speak slanderously against the Holy Father and the Church, pray for them, and speak only in kindness and in truth. Offer to everyone the words of Jesus Christ, that speak the truth, "... Upon you Peter, I will build My Church," to show them the institution of the first Pope, Leader and Shepherd, under Christ, for the whole Catholic Church, ... and ... "not even the gates of Hell will prevail against it," to show that my Son and I are always watching over the faithful and the servants of the Church. The Holy Spirit is constantly instilling peace, grace and virtue ... and the Father in Heaven is constantly guiding His Church with His hand of peace and love. My children, open your hearts and believe ... I leave you now in the peace of Almighty God.

* In a private message to Michael, Our Lady said that we could give the chaplet the name The Chaplet of Truth and Unity because it is for the unity of all the priests, religious, and faithful that we are praying, as well as for the strength of the truth of the Church, that it may live in the hearts of all men and women.

FEBRUARY 19, 1993 (JESUS) — My child, why are you troubled? Do you not know that I am with you at every moment? Would I let My work be destroyed or stopped by the evil one? This is why I have given you the Chaplet of Truth , so that many souls, who in the future will carry a greater cross, will have the strength to come to Me and to know that I direct and sustain souls through My Church. My children, do not doubt your Lord and His works. They are all for the good of your souls. They are all out of love. I leave you now with My peace and My blessing.

FEBRUARY 22, 1993 — My children, be humble, pure and charitable towards your neighbor. My children, love one another and forgive each other. Be reconciled with all those in your lives. My children, during this time of Lent I ask you to open your hearts in a greater way to my Son and allow Him to fill you with His light and His peace. My children, I love you so much and this is why I will continue to give you messages. Thank God, the Father, for this gift, that I am able to be with you for all this time. Pray, my children, and allow my love and my Son's love to fill your hearts, thus molding you into children of God. My children, again I say to you that it is a great gift that I am with you. Do not forsake the love of the Father, but be open to His will in your lives. I leave you now in the peace of God.

FEBRUARY 22, 1993 - SECOND MESSAGE — You, my child, be humble at all times. Be my little angel.

FEBRUARY 24, 1993 — I am very pleased with my priest-sons' decision to bring my Son, Jesus, out of the tabernacle to be solemnly exposed, so that my children may come to adore their God and receive His love and His mercy. Pray, my child, for the priests. Satan works tirelessly to destroy their holy vocations. Pray, pray, pray. Come before my Son, present in the Eucharist, and receive the outpouring of grace.

*This message refers to Michael's pastor and his decision to begin Perpetual Exposition of the Blessed Sacrament.

MARCH 10, 1993 — My dear child, please write for me. It has been some time since I gave you the last message. I wish you and all of my children to know that I have not abandoned you. I am always with you. My children, the world grows darker and so I ask you with tears in my eyes to pray the Holy Rosary and the Chaplet that I have given you. The Church prepares now for its greatest trial.

Pray, my children, and be a light to all those within your lives. Seek God's will in your daily actions. Only in this way, my children, will you find peace. Go now in the peace of God. Tell your spiritual directors that I am with them and am guiding them. They should not fear as the hour approaches, but should continue to lead my little ones along the path of love and peace.

MARCH 10, 1993 - SECOND MESSAGE — My children, offer up each little cross, with love, to my Son, for the salvation of souls and for the conversion of mankind.

MARCH 10, 1993 - THIRD MESSAGE — You will know why I have asked so much for prayer when the hour comes.

MARCH 18, 1993 — My dear child, I wish that the Chaplet of Truth be prayed every Thursday. On this day many graces will come forth and fill the hearts of my children. It will be a great remedy for the evil of sin and the attack which Satan puts forth against the Church. My children, pray and open your hearts. I desire the chaplet to be prayed on Thursday because it was on Holy Thursday that my Son gave to you the gift of Himself, truly present in the Holy Eucharist; as well, my Son instituted the Holy Priesthood on this night. Many hearts will be healed and conversions will take place through your prayer of the chaplet.

* One should not feel overwhelmed by what Our Lady asks — the Rosary, the Divine Mercy Chaplet, and the Chaplet of Truth. It is important mainly to make time for God and for prayer. If you are not able to find time to pray all of these, do not feel that you are doing any less. It is important to pray always for the priests, religious, and for the Church, no matter how you are praying. Our Lady has specifically asked for us to pray the chaplet on Thursday. Nothing is forced. Our Lady only invites us to pray we — are *asked* to open our hearts little by little. Our Lord and Our Lady will do the rest.

MARCH 23, 1993 (JESUS) — My child, for three days I desire that you come before Me in prayer at the hour of My death to offer as a sacrifice your prayer for My beloved son, John Paul, the shepherd of My Church. Pray with great intensity and love, and as a well-spring bursting forth, I shall fill your soul with divine grace. Pray for My Church which is now upon Calvary. Sacrifice and atone for the indecency and apostasy committed by My most precious ones.

MARCH 23, 1993 SECOND MESSAGE — My Child, do not fear what you cannot foresee. Trust in my Son and in me and in the inspirations that come to your heart from the Holy Spirit. Trust, my child and pray.

MARCH 24, 1993 (JESUS) — Come to My heart and seek refuge.

APRIL 5, 1993 — My child, please write for me. I am with you, present at every moment. Do not fear the enemy and his wiles. I am here to protect you and lead you ever to the gates of Paradise, to my Son and the peace and love which flows so abundantly from His Most Sacred Heart. My child, let my children know that there is no need to continue running to where I am appearing. I have said already, that if need be, I would appear in every house so that my precious little ones would be saved. It is sufficient for them to live my message. Come before my Son, truly present in the consecrated Host, in the tabernacle where He waits day and night for souls to come to Him to seek refreshment. It is there that they will find the Mother of All Mankind. It is there where they will find me present, because it is to my Son that I lead souls ... it is in Him that they will find salvation. I come to lead you all to Him and to Paradise.

Live the messages, my children, and do not be so preoccupied to find the people to whom I am appearing. Your Mother is with all of you. I am with each and every one of you. Open your hearts and there, in the recesses of your soul, in that silence, you will find your Mother ready to spark and thus ignite a fiery love for Jesus, the Son of God and Redeemer of Man.

APRIL 6, 1993 — My Children, I do not wish to admonish you. Again I ask you to pray with great fervor because time is precious. Each Hail Mary said with love helps to save souls. My children, you are so very dear to me. I ask you again to be open to my call, to listen to what I am asking of you. Again, I call you to live the messages. You will know why I have come so frequently. I leave you in the peace and joy of this time. Remember, my children, to go before the Cross and to meditate on the Passion of Jesus. Without the Cross there is no resurrection. Carry your crosses with patience and they will, in time, blossom into fragrant roses, thus representing the state of your soul. Pray for courage and for strength, my little ones. I leave you now, go in peace.

APRIL 7, 1993 — Oh my little one, be diligent in the spreading of my messages. Many of my children have not heard the voice of their Mother. Pray very much for them and for those who have heard my call and have not responded.

Pray the Rosary and be at peace. My Spouse will fill your heart with the knowledge of what to do in time.

I am leading you. Continue along the path of salvation. Live the message of the Gospel and stay close to my Son. He waits for you to bring your heart to Him and to present your worries. Oh, my children, how much my Son and I do love you! Open the eyes of your soul and you will come to know the great warmth of this eternal love. My precious ones, do you love me? Then please adhere to my warnings. Peace is not found in the heart of man and so I ask you, with great seriousness and with the love of a Mother, to pray and live for peace. Pray, my children. In prayer you will come to know the answers to many of your obstacles and problems. I leave you now. Your Mother loves you.

MAY 12, 1993 — My children, seek to end unrest, impurity, injustice, and all evil with your actions of purity, peace and prayer.

Change will come only when you respond to me with sincerity and with love. Only when you open your hearts to your Mother can she then transform you and present you, renewed, to Jesus. My children, open your hearts so that your inner beauty may shine forth and the splendor of the Trinity pour out as a well-spring from your hearts. This Mother desires greatly the conversion and renewal of her children, ... do not sadden me by refusing the love of your Mother.

MAY 28, 1993 — My dear little ones, today I call upon you to come before my Son, truly present in the Holy Eucharist. Come with love in adoration. Come and make reparation for the ingratitude of men and the incalculable number of sins with which humanity floods itself daily. My children, this most powerful means of prayer and reparation, before my Son, is a last means that I give to you. My children, I have already warned you and told you of the seriousness of what awaits you if mankind does not return to God. Pray especially during your Holy Hour for life, that abortion may end and that those involved with this grievous sin will be reconciled with God. My children, this sin marks humanity with a sore like no other. If you only knew my sorrow and the sorrow of my Son because of your destruction of life. Your lack of respect for the gift that the Father has given is what continues to draw you even further into the abyss of desolation and sorrow. Until this is reconciled you will continue to be immersed in darkness. If you do not desire to repent of your ways, then God's hand of justice will fall upon the earth. My children, if you only realized what destruction you are causing: the greatest of which is your lack of love for one another. You have lost love. My children, return to God and allow your Mother to once again teach you to love; to love life, to love God, and to love one another. Go in God's peace, my little ones.

JUNE 28,1993 — My dear children, today I exhort all of you to take into your hands that most predilected prayer of mine, the Holy Rosary. May your prayer of the Rosary fill you with peace and teach you the way of salvation. May your Rosary bind Satan and thwart all of the plans he has set for you. May you find my Son, Jesus, and the love of your Mother by your prayer of the Most Holy Rosary. My children, in these times I call upon you to consecrate yourselves and your families to my Son's Sacred Heart and to my Immaculate Heart. My children, I call you also to come in adoration before my Son, Jesus, Who is truly present in the Holy Eucharist. Before Him you will find me and we will lead you to the springs of peace and joy. I am the Mother of love, hope, and joy and I have come in these times to lead all of my children back to my Son, Jesus. My children, recognize my call and respond with open hearts. I love you all and I leave you in the peace of my Son.

JULY 9, 1993 — My dear child, please write for me. My little ones, all of you, please listen to your Mother, who now calls you with such love and tenderness; but my children, my message is very serious. Amidst this trial that you are now living through, many of you have not listened to my call and you continue to walk and live in what seems to be a perpetual darkness. Immorality is so widespread, with abortion continually being propagated, contraception practiced relentlessly and all unnatural forms of sexuality being practiced. My children, your souls are running the greatest risk of being eternally lost. Satan greatly desires to take you away from my Son. Do not allow him to do this. Turn away from all evil and ways of sin. Look upon my tears and the wounds of my Son and allow yourself to be moved to action. My children, tirelessly I tell you that your world is at the abyss. This is why I continue to call you to come back to God. Pray, my children. Make time for God so that in that time, that you give Him, He may speak to your heart and thus a conversion can begin. If you do not make time for God, He cannot help you. My children, seek the light of Christ. Go to Mass. Return to frequent Confession, thus unburdening yourself of the enormous weight of sin. Pray the Holy Rosary and follow the laws of God. The trial will continue to become harder. Seek the light, my little ones, and you will no longer be in darkness. Go in the peace of my Son.

JULY 13, 1993 — My dear little one, have I not traced out every part of your life with my Son? You must trust us more and know that everything is part of the plan that God has for you. Continue to walk the path of sanctity, of purity, humility, and a great love of prayer. Do not allow yourself anymore to be taken away from me by the lures of the world. I will lead you to my Son. Take my hand, my littlest of children, and have unbreaking faith in me, your Mother, and the Mother of All Mankind. I will not fail you. Go in God's peace, my little one.

JULY 22, 1993 — My dear children, it is my desire that you come to my maternal heart and solemnly consecrate yourselves and your families to my Immaculate Heart.

My children, I ask this of you because of the seriousness of these times. My children, I call upon you to renew your desire to live my messages and to place God first in your lives. Do not hesitate to decide for God and thus for what is good. Decide, my children, to do what is right in all situations and then you will see peace come into your hearts and your lives. Pray, my children, to know the will of God in your lives. Go in the peace of my Son.

JULY 29, 1993 — My dear children, at this time Satan works tirelessly for the ruin of souls. I implore you to listen to me and to the message I now bring. You are ever closer to the events which for some time now I have warned you of; for this reason and for the salvation of your souls, I ask you again to take the Rosary into your hands and to pray it. My children, do not continue to make excuses, but act with seriousness in your decision for God. Do not mock my Son. He sees and knows all that you do. Believe, my little ones, and pray for the conversion of sinners and for the unbelievers. I wish only to help you understand the importance of my presence among you. Do not continue to turn away, but instead listen and act upon my words. My children, seek God's will and in this way you will find peace. If you continue to walk the paths of pride, impurity, and materialism, then you will find only restlessness in your hearts. Listen, my children, and respond.

The time of great mercy is now here, and it shall come like the dawn, spreading its light over all of you. Also, though, God's justice awaits the command to fall upon the sinful world. In time you will understand this more clearly. The secrets are on the verge of coming to pass. The time of the Triumph of My Immaculate Heart is on the point of arriving. Again, I ask you to consecrate yourselves and your families to my Son's Sacred Heart and to my Immaculate Heart. We will be your protection amidst the great trial which now intensifies.

My child, pray and ask all of my little ones to pray. I leave you now in the peace of my Son.

AUGUST 3, 1993 — My dear children, today I come to you under the title of Our Lady of Grace and Mercy. I desire, my children, that you offer to your Immaculate Mother nine days of prayer for the conversion of sinners and in reparation for the great scourge of abortion. My little ones, I come to ask you to pray one mystery of the Most Holy Rosary and one Chaplet of Divine Mercy for nine consecutive days, beginning on the eve of the Feast of my Assumption into Heaven and ending on the Feast of the Queenship of your Mother, to bring down a flood of grace and mercy upon your country and the world. On this final day I will present your prayers to my Son, asking Him for the graces necessary for the world. I call upon you, my children, to join me in the battle against our adversary, Satan. My little ones, pray to change the events of the world. Please, respond to my call of prayer. Go in the peace of my Son, my little ones.

AUGUST 11, 1993 — My dear children, pray. If you but knew the events that have been altered forever by your prayer of the Rosary you would not even hesitate to pray all fifteen decades of it everyday. Through this simple prayer you give your Mother great power to intercede for you, for families, and for nations. Take the Rosary into your hands, my children, and make it an important priority of your everyday activities. I come to ask you to pray, not out of fear of what awaits you if you do not, but out of your love for me and my Son, Jesus. You should pray out of love and not out of fear. I love you all, my little ones.

SEPTEMBER 30, 1993 — It is in this way that I wish you to pray. To save more souls much more prayer is needed. My children, I ask you to consecrate more of your time for prayer. In this way you will receive a bountiful amount of graces. Souls are in great need of prayer.

OCTOBER 2, 1993 — My dear children, today I come to you in a very special way. I come full of joy because of the prayers and sacrifices of so many of my little ones. I ask you, though, to continue on still. Continue to offer to your Mother every sacrifice, even if it is little. If you offer it to me with love, then it becomes a great sacrifice.

My children, again today, I come to ask you to make reparation for the sins of the world. Especially, my children, I ask you to pray for those who have no one to pray for them. Go in the peace of My Son.

OCTOBER 11, 1993 — My children, confusion fills the heart of man. Today's world teaches you to do what feels good. I tell you that each of you is given a cross to bear from my Son. This cross is a great gift from Him. Some of you have heavier crosses than others; in this I ask you to persevere and know that My Son and I are with you. My children, do not be led astray into this darkness that now fills the Church and the world. Follow the truth which is set forth by the teaching of My Son's Church. If He were to physically come before you to speak the truth to you from His own mouth, would you then still mock Him? Then do not mock my beloved son, John Paul. My children, live the truth and you will be free from the snares set by my adversary. His time is coming to an end, and so again I beg you, do not join the darkness by living in sin, but choose to follow my Son. The greater trial is yet to come. Strengthen yourselves through the sacraments and through prayer. Go in the peace of My Son, my little ones.

OCTOBER 13, 1993 — My dear children, I come to you seeking a sincere response, still though, so many of you laugh at my mediation for you. You continue to act as if I have not appeared and have not warned you. My children, you have fallen deep into the mire of sin and thus your response to me is tepid. Your lives amidst the coming trials will be altered forever. Many of you will lose not only your earthly lives but your souls as well. Satan has set many traps for you and is continuing to do so. I tell you urgently to awaken to this present darkness and to seek the light of My Son. I intercede for each one of you before the throne of God. I will continue to do this, but I tell you, the time of mercy granted by God for the world is already ending. You are seeing this with the continuous uprising of war, both domestically and internationally. The Father will continue to allow this until you become aware of His call. Return to Him and the ways which He has set for you through His only Son, Jesus Christ. My children, become aware of the events in your world and of the increase of immorality. Do not remain so blind, following the ways of the world, for the world as you know it is coming to an end. You cannot continue in this darkness, and so My Son is about to fully unleash the justice of Heaven, and all the world will be renewed. My children, praise God in His goodness and mercy. Respond to my call, my children. This message is again to seriously warn you of the danger you are in and the need for conversion. Go in peace, my little ones.

*Our Lady was very sad but also very serious when she gave this message. She allowed me to understand and feel the loss of God; to lose grace and be out of favor in His eyes. What I experienced was *barely* the full reality of it. When I think of the souls who may be eternally lost in Hell, I am filled with an overwhelming sorrow. This is why we must pray very much for the unbelievers — those who do not know the love of God and those who refuse His love — for ourselves and for the further conversion of all sinners.

OCTOBER 15, 1993 — It was midnight — the beginning of the 15th of October — when I felt a very strong calling to go and pray before Our Lord. (There is a chapel nearby which has a seven-day-a-week, twenty-four-hour Exposition of the Blessed Sacrament.) I went to the chapel and knelt before Our Lord for about forty-five minutes. It was during this time that I was filled with such a great joy. I almost could not get up — my soul desired to continue to kneel before Him. The joy continued to grow in my heart to the point of overflowing. (This is the best way that I can describe it.) It was then that Our Lord spoke. Each word was powerfully felt within me, as if time began to move slower.

He said, **"It is here that I wish for you to come and rest. It is here that I will refresh you. Tell Me that you love Me to make up for the ingratitude of so many of My children in the world."**

At this point I began to say over and over again very slowly, "I love you, Jesus ... I love you, Jesus ..." I have never felt such a joy before. I wanted to be with Him for hours in that moment. I continued to kneel for a while more, telling Jesus that I loved Him and asking Him to have mercy on me and on all the world.

NOVEMBER 3, 1993 — My dear children, in the time to come the world will be shaken. All will come to pass for the purification of a world filled with sin and covered in darkness. This is why I have come, so many times, to repeat to you and urge you on to conversion. So many of you, my children, have allowed yourselves to be trapped by Satan by continually giving in to temptation. I call you to take the first step out of the darkness. I call you to pray and ask my Son for forgiveness so that He may free you from the shackles of sin. My children, what can I say that I have not already told you, to make you realize the importance of my messages? I can only say again: look to heaven. Listen to my words and begin to live them. In this way the light of My Son will fill your hearts and lives. Then you will begin to see the dawn of the new Era of Peace which is on the point of arriving. The year which is now so very close will be, in a greater way, the beginning of God's justice and a further time of His mercy. And so, my children, again I say to you; convert.

Do not wait to see the events which will take place, but begin now to love Jesus and to live in His light. I love you all, my little ones. Call upon me at this time and I will be your sure refuge as these days of yours begin to become more difficult to live in. Hope in the Lord, Who has not abandoned you. I am the great sign pointing the way back to God. Do not turn away from me, my children, but take your Mother's hand. I am here for you.

NOVEMBER 14, 1993 — My dear children, today I come to you as the Mother of the Church. I ask you to pray fervently and to offer up many sacrifices for the good of the Church and for those within, who have fallen away from my Son. My children, I suffer greatly because of my priest-sons who mock my Son and the truths of the Church. Pray very much for them.

Open your hearts, my little ones. Be open to the love of Jesus. I have warned you enough, already. I tell you at this time, believe and live lives worthy of God. Do not continue to walk in the darkness, but walk into the light. My Son is calling you. I love you, my children. Again ... please, pray for the Church ... her hour has arrived.

* Michael said that it was with great love that Our Lady said, "I have warned you enough, already." Our Lady does not wish to continually admonish us, but she wishes for us to realize, very seriously, the urgency and importance of her presence with us and the messages that she has given to us.

NOVEMBER 14, 1993 - SECOND MESSAGE — It has been your prayer before the Blessed Sacrament these many Sundays that has secured for you Perpetual Adoration. Use well the gift My Son has given you.

* In this message Our Lady is speaking about the Sunday night prayer group in Michael's parish. Since April 26, 1992, upon the Blessed Mother's request, there has been Exposition of the Blessed Sacrament during the prayer group.

NOVEMBER 16, 1993 — The Rosary is especially the weapon I give to you. Use it, my children. If you could only see what is to come and the need for prayer and sacrifices for the many who may be lost eternally. My children, again I repeat to you: convert and decide for God. The times of mercy are here ... now. Do not let them pass by with a response of weariness. Follow my call with great love. If you do, you will come into the light. My Son and I are with you always. Go in the peace of God, my little ones.

NOVEMBER 19, 1993 — My children, continue to pray and walk the path of conversion. Thank Almighty God for the graces that He has poured out upon you. Seek to please my Son. Turn away from all that is useless and all that takes you away from Jesus. Thank you, my children, for responding to me with joy. My children, spread this joy, which my Son gives to you. Give it freely to others.

NOVEMBER 21, 1993 - FEAST OF CHRIST THE KING — How much joy you have given my heart on this day. How pleased I am with my beloved son who has said yes to my Son, Jesus. A thousandfold will your parish and the many souls who come here receive graces. How abundant will be the outpouring of mercy from Jesus. My children, please continue to say "yes" to Jesus. Continue to open your hearts and love my Son, Jesus, in the Most Blessed Sacrament. I am with you.

* On this day in Michael's parish Perpetual Eucharistic Adoration began. Our Lady's words, "my beloved son", refer to the pastor of the church. Our Lady allowed Michael to feel some of her great joy because of Perpetual Adoration. Michael said, "It is too powerful for words to express. Our Mother in heaven greatly desires us to adore Jesus in the Blessed Sacrament. This is the beginning sign of the Triumph of Her Immaculate Heart. It is needed for us to further our conversion and to make reparation for the sins of the world. Perpetual Adoration is a great means of bringing mercy upon the world."

DECEMBER 7, 1993 — My dear children, this is a time of great grace. I ask you to be open and to respond to this time that God has given to you. My children, God has given you something wonderful in allowing me to be with you this long, but the time is coming when this will no longer be. I do not wish for you to be sad, but to be full of hope and joy. If you listen and live the messages that I am bringing to you then your hearts will be filled with joy, but if you remain closed to the graces of this present time then you cannot experience this joy.

I implore you, my little ones, to be open to the call of your Mother and to say "yes" to Jesus in your lives. Be at peace, my children, and know that I am with you now in a special way.

DECEMBER 8, 1993 - THE FEAST OF THE IMMACULATE CONCEPTION — How greatly my heart is wounded by the ingratitude of my children. The selfish sins of my children are those which cause divorce, abortion and my endless tears. My children, repair for the numerous sins of the world. The Father in Heaven is greatly angered over the sins of the world. A time of terrible suffering awaits you, my children. This is why I have come: to warn you and to show you the path of peace. Some of you have listened, but many of you have not. In a short time events will occur which will shake the world and cause humanity to see what it has done.

I plead with you, though, not to wait for that time, but to begin your conversion now. I am waiting for you and desire greatly to help you, but I cannot unless you say "yes." My children, say yes and through your "yes" console our hearts and begin walking the path of salvation. I am the Immaculate Conception. I am the Queen of Peace. I have come, my children, to bring light to this world of darkness. Go and begin living the messages with words and actions. I am with you.

* Our Lady says to us in this message, "I plead with you to begin your conversion now. I am waiting for you and desire greatly to help you,

but I cannot unless you say 'yes.'" She sees what awaits us if we do not live her messages. Not only sorrow here on earth, but as well, and more importantly, the possibility of our losing our souls forever.

She tells us, "Some of you have listened, but many of you have not." How many of us try and spread this message of conversion only to find a response of complete disinterest? How many of us know in our hearts how serious Our Lady's message is and yet even we do not live it day in and day out? This is why she speaks powerfully in this message (as in others). She wishes for us to know how important it is that we open our hearts and begin to place Jesus in the center of our lives. At the end of this message, she again repeats to us, "Go and begin living the messages with words and actions. I am with you." Our Lady continues to call us. She points out that we have the free-will to decide what is to happen to us. God comes to give us His light and His peace. Satan comes to bring us into the darkness and unrest into our hearts. We have the choice. Everyday we are confronted with good and evil. Everyday we have many chances to decide for God or for Satan. Our Lady is telling us that to have peace we must decide for God. Our Lady is with us to guide and protect us. It is up to us to say "yes" to her. It is up to us to say yes to Jesus Christ.

Let us, each day, say "yes" to Jesus in our lives. Let us say yes to the light and to peace. Let us open our hearts.

DECEMBER 10, 1993 — How strongly I ask my priest-sons that they strictly observe their vow of celibacy and that they work ardently toward the virtue of purity! My little one, pray for all of my priest-sons and religious, and exhort others to pray for them as well.

DECEMBER 13, 1993 - MESSAGE FROM ST. MICHAEL THE ARCHANGEL — The Virgin desires the conversion of the greatest number. Seek God's mercy. Seek to be children of God, and then you will be marked. Console the Hearts of Jesus and Mary through prayer and sacrifices.

In an interior vision Michael saw St. Michael before him. St. Michael's hands were together in prayer and his eyes were raised to Heaven. A sword of light, which seemed to be of fire, was in mid-air in front of St. Michael. When St. Michael spoke the words, "Seek to be children of God, and then you will be marked," an illuminated cross appeared above the angel's head.

DECEMBER 18, 1993 — My child, let me speak to you of what is to come. The world must be purified of its sin, this is why God will allow chastisements to come amidst the purification. Humanity will have a time of light before greater events take place. The world will know that God is calling. People will see themselves, their souls, and will be given the chance, in a great way, to change and to lead lives of holiness, and not lives of sin, as many are doing now.

The world is cloaked in a great darkness. Satan seems to have his victory, but this is not so. My Son and I are with you. My Son is filling hearts with His mercy, with His light. I have come to call mankind; to awaken the world. If you could only realize the full reality of your situation. The ever-increasing danger you see around you is a sign that change is needed. That change is for you to return to God and to begin to live lives full of faith and love.

I come particularly in these days as the Mother of Hope, because it is the hope of Jesus that I bring to this world, which is filled with despair. My children, look to my Son and open your hearts. Begin to take little steps toward Jesus. In this way, my little ones, you will find the light and you will be saved. For peace to come, the world must change.

I come to bring hope, my children. Live this hope; do not live in despair. Allow my Son to cleanse you and to fill your hearts of darkness with the light of His mercy and love. Go, my children. Do not be afraid, but begin now, as the new year approaches. Begin to allow Jesus to work within your hearts and thus transform your lives of confusion into lives of peace and love. Go in God's peace, my little ones.

DECEMBER 21, 1993 — My love for the first of my beloved sons is so very great. I ask you to continue to pray for him (Pope John Paul II) and to offer up your communions for his strength and perseverance. He is my gift to you. He is your light in the Church amidst the ever increasing darkness which envelops it.

My children, realize the moment that you live in. You are all being called to decide; to decide for God or for sin and death. My children, listen to your Mother and begin anew each day to live the Gospel message and to love my Son, Jesus, more and more. Prepare, in a special way, for this new year and throughout the new year for the times that await you. You will need to continue to strengthen your faith and love for Jesus. Do this through the sacraments and through the Rosary. Do not continue to live habitually in sin, in mortal sin, but go to Confession and begin to walk the path that leads to Paradise. Do not continue in the darkness, aimlessly following the path of eternal damnation. My children, this Mother desires that you change your lives. Allow my Son to transform you into budding and then blossoming flowers of virtue and holiness. I am here in a special way, in these days, to protect you and to guide you. Have recourse to me. I will lead you to Jesus. I love you all. Go in God's peace.

DECEMBER 22, 1993 — My children, if you do not open yourselves then I cannot help you. Each day you must open your hearts more and try each day to love Jesus and those around you. This means to persevere in the trials of everyday life; to live in patience and with peace and to help others overcome their difficulties through prayer and good works. My children, open yourselves and be a light to those around you. Prepare now, in a special way, for the day of light has arrived. I am with you. Wait and prepare in holy silence.

* Again, Our Lady says, with love, that we must say "yes" — we have our own free will to say "yes" or "no." God will not force us to be holy and to lead good lives. She says, "Prepare for the 'day of light' (Christmas) in holy silence." She means that we need to be joyful not only on the outside with others (family and friends) but be awaiting this wonderful day with great joy and anticipation within our hearts as well.

DECEMBER 31, 1993 — My dear children, the year 1994 has arrived. Today, on the very eve of the new year, I repeat to you again the great need for prayer and conversion. I come with joy and with sorrow. I come with joy because the time of peace is coming; with each passing day its arrival draws nearer. As well, I am filled with sorrow because of what you will live through in order for the Triumph of my Heart to come. I have forewarned of the great danger the world is in and again today I tell you that justice is coming. The justice of God will become even more clear in this year. This is why I urge all of you on to conversion.

OPEN YOUR HEARTS

My children, in this year, 1994, I ask you in a most serious way to look deep into your hearts and to begin to root out all which does not allow you to come closer to Jesus. Take out all that brings darkness and destroys the light. Open yourselves to the love and mercy of Jesus. I ask you again to pray the Rosary with your hearts. Do not pray it because you feel you have to but because you want to. If you do not then it will begin to be a burden for you and you will slowly lose the peace that God has given you. Satan, as well, will begin to conquer in your hearts. Allow the Rosary to fill you with the grace you need to walk the path of holiness in these days.

I ask that you foster great devotion for my Son, who is truly present in the Holy Eucharist. Prepare for Mass and open your hearts during the Mass, my children. Come before my Son in hours of adoration to bring down graces upon yourselves, your country and the world. Love Jesus in the Most Blessed Sacrament.

My children, in this year, try and begin to love Jesus and each other more. Do not allow Satan to fill your hearts with hatred for God and for one another. Open your hearts and allow the sacraments to strengthen you on your journey. I am always with you, my children. Go and be loving children of God.

MESSAGES FROM THE YEAR 1994

JANUARY 14, 1994 — My children, come before my Son, who is truly present in the Most Blessed Sacrament. There, before Him, in hours of adoration you will receive the graces needed to be true followers of Christ. There, before this Sacrament of Love, you will be refreshed and you will find peace amidst the confusion of your lives.

My children, I urge you to pray and to make hours of adoration and reparation before my Son, in the Most Holy Sacrament of the Altar. Come to Jesus, who wishes so much to transform your lives. Come, my little ones, before the Light of the World.

MARCH 3, 1994 — My dear children, again today I call you to pray and to bring peace to those around you. Pray for peace to come into the hearts of all men and women. My children, do not think that peace will come through the arrangements of world leaders. Peace will only come when mankind places God at the center of life. Until that time man will continue to bring destruction and death upon himself. In this year and in those to come, seeds of death and unrest will continue to be sown by Satan.

My children, live by the laws of God and not by the laws of man. I ask you again, to be children of God ... and again I tell you that events lie ahead that will cause great changes in the world and in the lives of many. Seek the light, my little ones. There you will find Jesus, Who is the truth. In Jesus you will find peace. Go and be bearers of the peace that Jesus gives you. I love you, my little ones.

* Our Lady again asks us to pray for peace, but as well, to be bearers of peace. All of us need to start in our own lives. We need to look at ourselves and work on living peace. This means to be Christ-like to others. We ask Jesus to forgive us and to grant us His peace, but we, as well, need to be forgiving and peaceful with others. Our Lady tells us, "In Jesus you will find peace. Go and be bearers of the peace that Jesus gives you." Our Lady talks of the reality of Satan and his influence in the world, but she desires us not only to pray for peace in the world but to work for that peace in our own lives. This is why she has come: to bring Jesus into our lives so that not only our lives, but, also, the world, will change and find peace. The peace, she says, which only Christ can give.

MARCH 25, 1994 - FEAST OF THE ANNUNCIATION — Praised be Jesus, my children. On this glorious day I ask that you, with me, say your "yes" to God. Open your hearts anew today, my little ones, and allow God to work within your lives. I am with you all, my children.

Continue to recite the chaplet that I have given you. See the graces it brings forth upon the Church. Many, many souls who are lost in the mire of sin will be cleansed and brought forth again, in grace, through this prayer of love for the Church. Go in the peace of my Son and may your hearts be filled with a special joy on this day.

In a vision Michael saw Our Lady, all in white (as he has seen her before). She was leaning over and looking down. In her right hand was a beautiful clear crystal rosary and as Michael recited the Chaplet of Truth it seemed that tiny jewels (which looked like diamonds or crystals) were falling in abundance from Our Lady's Rosary. Michael then saw a priest who's priestly clothes were very dirty and who's face was discolored with dark smudges. As the jewels of grace fell upon him from the Rosary his face and his clothes became very clean until the priest was almost aglow. Michael then saw a lay person hunched over, filled with sadness, and as the jewels fell upon her she rose up out of her position and began to smile and cry with joy.

Finally, Michael saw a woman who was kneeling down, praying, and as the tiny jewels fell upon her she, filled with a great peace, looked up to Heaven and her face beamed with love for God.

The vision of Our Lady and then the three successive visions were given to show the graces received from praying the chaplet.

MAY 13, 1994 - FEAST OF OUR LADY OF THE MOST BLESSED SACRAMENT — My child, may your heart be ever open that I may touch your soul with the graces of my Son. Fear not but continue on the path which has been set for you. I am always with you. Especially today I thank you and tell you that I will protect and guide you in a special way because of your promise to me. I am your Mother and the Mother of all. Continue to pray the Holy Rosary and to come before my Son, truly present in the Most Blessed Sacrament. Entreat others to do the same so that their lives can be renewed and transformed into lives of peace and grace. My children, come to me with your troubles. I will comfort you and lead you all to Jesus, Lord and Savior; King of Kings. Trust in God and His infinite mercy. My little ones, live in the truth of God. Go now in the peace of my Son.

JUNE 1, 1994 — My dear children, today, again, I come to ask you to open your hearts and to decide seriously for God. This world continues in its sin and in its obstinacy against the ways of God. My little ones, look to Jesus and your confusion will be no more. My Son awaits you. He awaits your 'yes'. He waits patiently for you to open your hearts to Him. He loves you and desires your return. My children, for many years now I have been slowly guiding you; forming your hearts in prayer and in love. As well, I have warned you of the danger that is possible and that which will come.

My children, seek joy and peace and do not dwell on punishment. God loves you and wishes only good things for you. All that may come and the salvation of your souls depends on you. Respond to my call with peace and with love. Do not be constantly worried with the things of the world but trust in Jesus. Trust, my children. Love one another, love God and accept that which He wants of you. His will is for the good of all mankind. Go in His peace.

JUNE 1, 1994 — My little one, write for me. These things I ask of you; prayer, penance, peace. To fulfill these and live them to the fullest degree, the sure path to strengthen you is prayer. Prayer, my children, will be your life's fire. Go to Holy Mass, opening yourselves to the great graces which flow forth from this Sacrifice of Love. Prayer of the Rosary; meditating on the life of Jesus. Prayer of the Scriptures. Read the Bible, my little ones. Keep the word of God in your hearts. It will teach you many things and will give you the strength to persevere in times of sorrow. I am with you, my children. Go in peace.

JUNE 14, 1994 - (JESUS) — This closeness which you feel toward this present Pope is a gift that I have given you. With this love that your heart is filled with, I ask also for sacrifice. Pray and sacrifice for My beloved son, My Vicar on earth. Go in My peace.

JUNE 22, 1994 — My dear child, come close to my heart and pray. Open yourself fully to the will of God, that His plans may be fulfilled in you. Live a holy life so that you may be a sign for others. All of you who wish to follow my Son and be children of God — be pure, humble and charitable. Persevere in faith and in grace. Be full of joy and give this joy to others. My little ones, consecrate yourselves to me with a renewed desire. Live the Commandments with a great love. Open your hearts to my Son and allow Him to teach you the ways of holiness. I love you all, ... go in His peace.

JULY 1, 1994 - FIRST FRIDAY — My dear little one, write for me. How much I love all of you, my children. How I have called you all to follow the road of love and peace in these years so that your souls may be placed in my heart, the refuge amidst this current storm. My children, you must continue to listen with humility and obedience to the voice of your Mother, who leads you to the Son, the Savior, the Lord and King; Jesus Christ. My little ones, today again, I ask that you walk in purity. In these times this virtue is constantly being plagued by fashions and current thoughts of how one should and can live. My children, you must see the truth from lies. Satan desires to lead you down the road of impurity and immodesty to secure your souls in darkness. Thus, if you begin to be weak in this area you will begin to fall in others. This is why I call you to ever be humble and obedient to the Church and her guidance in her teaching of the truth. Stay close to my beloved son, John Paul II. How much he pleases me in his constant love in following my Son.

My children, the hour of trials has arrived. I ask you then, to remain close to Jesus and to me, your Mother. Do not fear, but be filled with the hope that I bring at this time. Open your hearts and be filled with the peace of Jesus. Then you will persevere and in time come to eternal joy when your journey has ended. My children, know with certainty that I am with you and that Jesus loves you. Go in peace, my children.

JULY 1, 1994 - SECOND MESSAGE — My child, hear my call for you to sacrifice and pray unceasingly for my littlest ones, who are being immersed into the diseased ocean of sexual sin and deviation. See them covered in the sores of shame and fear because of the grave sins of those around them. My child, see my heart and the heart of my Son, pierced because of these horrible atrocities against the children; against the Father in Heaven. Justice will be great for those who participate in these sins in any way. Michael pray, pray for them. Hold your Rosary up to our hearts and the balm of your prayers, the prayers of all my children and the cries of these little ones will make reparation, ease the pains of our hearts and lessen the just anger of God, the Father. My Son has allowed you to understand in a strong way the seriousness of these sins and the sadness of our hearts. Please, pray for them and make many sacrifices. May you respond to my call and be a victim of love and reparation for these littlest and dearest children of mine.

JULY 5, 1994 — My dear child, today again, I come to the world calling all to return to Jesus. I ask all of my children that they believe in my presence here and that they respond to my call. Little children, pray and open yourselves to the love of my Son, Jesus. Read the Bible everyday and in the sacred word find peace, strength and the wisdom to live lives of holiness. Continue on the road of perseverence and goodness. Continue to call upon me, your gentle and loving Mother. I come in these days as the Mother of Hope.

In these times of immense sorrow I come bringing the light of Christ. Oh, my children, if you only knew that I am so close to you with my Son. We are with you always. Open your hearts and allow the peace of God to enter. Trust in your Mother. I will lead you all to Jesus; to the light that you seek and so urgently need in this darkened world. I love you all.

AUGUST 26, 1994 — My children, continue to come before Jesus with a great love in your hearts. This infinite gift of His true presence with you. If you could only realize His love for you. Thank Him, my children, by loving Him in return. If souls could understand this gift of love ... an infinite love, a boundless gift from Jesus to all the world. In every tabernacle of the world my Son is truly present, awaiting your return. It is only your love that He seeks. Love Jesus, my children. Love Him with all that you have and thus discover the joy that He brings. Surrender yourselves and love one another. I love you all and I am with you. Go in God's peace.

AUGUST 26, 1994 - SECOND MESSAGE — My child, I will tell you the secret of holiness. Humbly love Jesus in the Most Blessed Sacrament. In Him is to be found everything.

SEPTEMBER 6, 1994 - (VISION IN PRAYER) — Inner vision of a priest kissing the first marble step leading up to the altar and from the base of a monstrance (from the altar) blood pouring forth in mercy/ graces (from the Blessed Sacrament exposed in the monstrance). With a pure white lamb at the base of the monstrance and a light coming forth from the Host, in all directions. (A soft, white light.)

SEPTEMBER 6, 1994 — My dear child, it is my desire that you open your heart fully to the love of my Son. Immerse yourself in prayer; a deeper prayer of the heart. Continue to do the will of God and work to attain the peace of my Son and the peace of your brothers and sisters. Love, forgive, and be merciful to all those you come in contact with. Be a bearer of love. Be a sign to those around you. I am with you always, my child.

SEPTEMBER 13, 1994 — The sins of the flesh cut deep into my heart and the heart of my Son. Pray and sacrifice for these children of mine who are in darkness and who are walking to the abyss. My children, you continue to do only what feels good to the flesh and not what is good. You ignore the truth of creation and walk in your own prideful ways. This is such a loss. A loss for your souls ... actions which have led and continue only to lead to a loss of life and love.

My children, follow the truth of my Son; the truth of the teachings of the Church. Go in peace, my little ones.

OCTOBER 8, 1994 - (JESUS) (WHILE PRAYING BEFORE THE TABERNACLE IN CHAPEL) — Michael, it is My desire that you come to visit with Me for one hour everyday. Come and console My heart with your love and I, in turn, will give you the peace and rest you seek. You will please Me very much in doing so.

OCTOBER 20, 1994 - OUR LADY — My dear child, write for me. You have been given many graces from above; all this time that my Son and I have been with you and the insight into the ways of God. My child, the work my Son has given to you is an important one. Continue to pray, make sacrifices and be a merciful servant of the Lord. Bring the light of my Son to the world through your words and actions. Lift up your prayers to me with love, my little one, for those whom you have been asked to pray for. Ease our hearts in doing so. Your prayers will be heard. Thank the Lord everyday for all that He has done for you.

I ask that each day all of you, my children, read a passage from Scripture and, meditating on the word of God, allow Him to touch your hearts. Go in peace, my dear little ones.

OCTOBER 24, 1994 — My child, be little and humble and love my Son with all your heart. Trust in Him always. Like a good son, place your hand in His and do not fear of what may come in life. We are always with you. Please, continue to pray and make sacrifices for those specific intentions that I have asked of you. Do not fear, my little one. Go in peace."

DECEMBER 5, 1994 — My dear little one, please ... write for me. How many souls have strayed from the heart of my Son and, thus, from my heart. How deep are the wounds caused by their refusal to love. Pray for them. Come before my Son and, with your prayers and your love, ease the pains which our hearts suffer through. Repair for the loss of love with your love.

There is a great need for souls to pray and make reparation for other souls who have become lost in the darkness of sin. With your prayers reach out and snatch these souls from the grip of the enemy. Pray and prepare each day for the coming of Jesus. I am with you, always.

DECEMBER 5, 1994 - SECOND MESSAGE — My child, you have felt the graces overwhelm your heart and overflow into your soul. Speak to others of the love that my Son has for *all* of His children. Come to the Light of the World. Come, my little ones, before Jesus, truly present in the Most Blessed Sacrament. He waits day and night for you. Come and find your rest.

DECEMBER 9, 1994 — My dear little one, ... I ask you to pray for those children of mine who feel that my Son has abandoned them. Pray that they may come to know His love and desire for reconciliation and for the beginning of their return to the truth.

My Son does not expect perfection. He asks only that you try with sincerity; that your intention be to follow Him. He will make up for what is lacking. In your sorrow He will comfort you; your tears He will wipe away; your sin-stained souls He will wash anew to dazzling purity in His most Precious Blood. My children, look into the eyes of my Son, our Lord and Savior, Jesus Christ, and see the love and mercy which He desires to fill you with. I, your Mother, am with you *always*. Place your hand in mine. I am waiting for you, to aid you in every way in finding, knowing and loving Jesus. My children, open your hearts to Him.

DECEMBER 14, 1994 — My dear children, the path which my Son asks you to walk is a simple one. It is the path of love. My little ones, love at the center of your lives will enable you to follow my Son in holiness and peace. It will give you the strength to walk to Calvary and to rise above the troubles of your days. Know, always, that I am with you. I am your Mother of Love. Come to me and I will open the heart of my Son for you when you fear that He has taken His eyes away from you.

My children, this is never so. My Son waits for each one of you with an unquenchable love. Do not fear to come into the heart of my Son where this fire burns.

My children, I will never tire in guiding you and pointing out the way which leads to the heart of Jesus, who is the King of all hearts. As a Mother, I desire only this; that you come to know and love my Son and thus love and forgive one another so that His peace may reign supreme in your hearts. My children, go and love Jesus and one another.

DECEMBER 24, 1994 — My children, rejoice with me today on the eve of the birth of my Son, the Savior of the World. Jesus, who comes to bring truth to all mankind. Jesus, who is the Light of the World and who wishes to lift men's hearts out of darkness and into the light. Jesus, who is mercy, comes to pour forth His love and His peace upon all the world. My children, on this night and in each day of your lives, allow my Son to bring His truth, His peace, His love and His light into your lives. Allow Jesus to transform your lives. I love you and I am with you in a special way on this night. Pray, my little ones ...

DECEMBER 30, 1994 — My children, as this year ends and the new year quickly approaches, I repeat to you again, be bearers of the light and of truth in your world, so filled with darkness and confusion. My children, bring the Truth of Jesus to all those around you. Be filled with the hope of Christ. I come as the Mother of Hope. Come one and all under my protective mantle of love. I call each one of you to love Jesus and to live good, holy lives. Be open to Jesus. Be open to the truth, my little ones.

DECEMBER 30, 1994 - (JESUS) - SECOND MESSAGE (RECEIVED WHILE IN PRAYER BEFORE THE BLESSED SACRAMENT) — Michael ... come to Me each day to console My heart which is greatly wounded by sin. Come to console Me with your love and your desire. Come and make reparation for the sins of man, for they are many. With your love, My child, make up for the ingratitude of men, who still today laugh at Me, mock Me, scourge Me, and crucify Me with their disbelief in My real presence. Even My closest companions, My priests, deny Me their friendship; their love. How greatly this hurts Me. Come and love Me, your Jesus. I wait for you, ... for all of you to come with your love. Bring Me your wounded hearts. Come to Me, My precious ones. Come to your Friend, who waits day and night for you, who is consumed with love for you. Come and let us love one another.

OPEN YOUR HEARTS

OPEN YOUR HEARTS

MESSAGES FROM THE YEAR 1995

JANUARY 5, 1995 — My dear little one, I ask you to pray fervently and to make many sacrifices for all of the children and youth in the world. For all those that are sick and suffering; mentally, physically and emotionally, and for all those children of mine who have fallen into the shadows of darkness. The darkness of pride, anger, materialism and sexual promiscuity and deviation. My child, with your prayers and your love in action and sacrifices help them. By your prayers many will return to my Son. By your prayers many who are lost will come into the light and be found. Many who are at the edge of the abyss will be saved through your loving prayers and acts of reparation. Be a powerful intercessor and friend of the children and youth of the world. Tell others to pray for them as well so that my adversary will be defeated in his plan to take them away from my Son and me. May Jesus reign supreme in your hearts, my little ones. For this to be possible you must open your hearts and invite Him into your lives. My children, open wide the door of your hearts so that you may come to know the love, mercy and peace of my Son, Jesus Christ. I love you all and I am with you.

JANUARY 19, 1995 — My dear child, I have come to you these many years to lead souls back to my Son, to encourage all, especially priests and consecrated souls to love and follow, in obedience, the Successor of Peter, and to adore my Son, TRULY present in the Most Blessed Sacrament. In the beginning I called you and all of my children slowly, but with urgency because of the danger humanity is in. I spoke of chastisement to warn you that the world must always follow God or risk serious problems, if it wishes to follow the lures of materialism and a self-centered value system.

If you do not follow Jesus, who is truth, then you risk being lost in lies and confusion. Much of the world has decided to walk upon this path instead of the one of my Son.

My children, I am the Mother of Hope. I have repeated this to you many times ... I come to lead you all to Jesus; the way, the truth and the life. Follow Him, always. Trust in Him, my little ones. He will never leave you. My children, be filled with hope and with peace. Many of you have decided to walk the path of goodness and love. I ask you to persevere and to lead others to Jesus by your upright words and actions. Be children of prayer ... always calling upon the Holy Spirit to fill your hearts and minds. Be children of the word and read the Bible everyday. It will be your teacher, your consoler and your strength. Most of all ... be children of the Eucharist. Realize with open hearts this gift which Jesus has given to the world. Love Jesus in the Blessed Sacrament.

Finally, my little ones, ... have frequent recourse to me, your Mother. I am here for you always, for each one of you. Do not hesitate, my little ones, to come to me. I wait for you. I will take your hand and gently lead you to my Son, the King of Kings, the Lord of Lords, the Prince of Peace; Jesus Christ. Open your hearts, my children, ... open them wide for Jesus.

JANUARY 23, 1995 — My children, why have I come to you here and in so many other places? It is to call you all back to God, ... the One, Triune God. My children, for this to happen you must be open to the love of my Son, which is the call of this Mother. I have come simply to awaken humanity. I have come to call all the world and this is why, particularly here, I have come as the Mother of All Mankind. Recall the words uttered by my Son, in His agony upon the Cross, "Behold your Mother ...," and so for centuries I have looked upon all of humanity as my children, and many of you have looked upon me as your Mother.

My children, again, in these days of yours, filled with confusion and darkness, I have come to call you to find and walk the path which leads to Jesus, who is the Way, the Truth and the Life. My little ones, I have been with you for many years, appearing again and again to many of you, to call you to prayer and to repentance. Again, I come bringing hope; Jesus Christ.

My children, hear the voice of your Mother, who calls you all with a great love; the love of my maternal and Immaculate Heart. Come into this refuge. Come into the light that brings hope amidst your despair, love amidst hatred, and peace in your days of endless confusion and anxiety. Return to the One, True, Almight God, who awaits the return of each one of you. Look into the eyes of my Son and see the love and mercy which awaits you. Look into the eyes of this Mother and see the maternal embrace which awaits you. Do not fear, but take the first step. Hear my call, my little ones. I love you and I am with you.

JANUARY 26, 1995 - (JESUS) (RECEIVED WHILE PRAYING IN THE CHAPEL BEFORE THE TABERNACLE) — My dear child, My Mother and I will not be with you, in this way, for much longer. Persevere in prayer and remember well the words that we have given you. In your times of sorrow and in joy come and visit Me. I love you with an unquenchable love. Trust in Me, always, and lead others to do the same. Open your heart and allow Me to pour forth, in abundance, My peace. Go forth, My child, in strength and in courage, knowing that I will always be at your side. I love you.

When Our Lord asks Michael to come and visit Him, He is speaking of His TRUE presence in the Blessed Sacrament in the tabernacle of our churches. He has consistantly called upon all of us, in these messages, to come and spend time with Him; to tell Him that we love Him and to thank Him for all that He has given to us. He greatly desires us to know and love Him in the Blessed Sacrament.

JANUARY 29, 1995 — My child, I come this night to be with you in a very special way ... to begin to prepare you for the time, which is now so very close, when I will not be with you as I have been in these past years. My Son and I are very pleased with you and with your desire to live a good, holy life. My child, continue to strive to follow Jesus every day.

My little one, these past years have been a special time for you; a time of infinite grace. I ask that you, beginning this night, pray and make many, little sacrifices to thank Jesus for this gift that He has given you; that we have been with you in this extraordinary way. My child, it is truly a great gift that you have been given and my Son and I are very pleased with your response and with the work you have done. Continue, each day, to be open to the work of the Holy Spirit in your life. Continue, each day, to spread the Gospel message with words and actions.

I ask, again, that all of my children participate in the Holy Sacrifice of the Mass with a great desire to meet Jesus, who comes to them in the Holy Eucharist. I call upon all of you to frequently go to Confession; to rid yourselves of sin and to gain the graces needed to live holy lives. Again, I ask you to read the Bible and allow the Holy Spirit to enlighten you and help to transform your life through the words of Scripture.

My child, this night you feel the love that I have for you and for all of my children and the great desires of my heart. Do not feel sorrow over what I have said to you. My Son and I will always be with you. In your times of joy and suffering, I will come to you bringing the hope and peace of Jesus. I have come here to you these many years to gently call all the world to love my Son, Jesus Christ.

My little one, ... do not be sad ... continue to prepare for your day of consecration to Jesus through the heart of your Mother. I will come to you on that day and lovingly accept and present your consecration to my Son. My child, may you continue to give great joy to my heart and the heart of my Son by loving Him always. My child, be at peace.

FEBRUARY 9, 1995 - (JESUS) — My child, simply, I ask you to love. Be humble and charitable. Forgive as I have forgiven.

FEBRUARY 10, 1995 - (JESUS) — My dear child, once again I ask you to come and spend time with Me. Ease the pains of My heart. Soothe the wounds of ingratitude with the balm of your love for Me. I thank you ... I love you with such sweet tenderness. My little one, be attentive to My voice ... hear Me when I call you. Follow Me, always. Love, always.

FEBRUARY 11, 1995 - FEAST OF OUR LADY OF LOURDES (LAST OF THE CENTRAL CORE MESSAGES GIVEN TO MICHAEL) — My little child, I come to you today for the last time. Do not be afraid ... my Son and I will always be with you. The time for me to be with you is completed ... ,many souls have greatly benefited from these graces and many more will continue to benefit from my Son's mercy.

My children, I am the Mother of all Mankind, ... *your* Mother. I love you all so much, and this is why I have come these many times to speak to you of my Son; to point the way to Him, to warn and encourage you. My children, ... penance and prayer. I have come to pour forth the light of Jesus in the places where there is darkness, ... to bring peace where there is unrest, and to bring the love of Jesus where there is hatred and violence. I have come, my children, with the hope of faith where there is doubt. My children, Jesus can heal all of your wounds. For all of your questions, He has the answer. In a world filled with lies and deception, He is the fullness of truth. Jesus Christ is the Savior of all Mankind. Look to Jesus. Love Jesus. Trust, always, in Jesus, my children.

Do not doubt but have faith in my presence here. Open your hearts and allow my Son to transform your lives. Open the doors of your lives to the Prince of Peace. My children, in your time of need turn to me, ... I will never fail to lead you to Jesus. I am your Mother, always desiring to help you to know, love and trust in Jesus Christ, the Redeemer of Mankind. I love you all ...

My little one, ... I love you ... Reach out and take my hand and continue to allow me, each day, to take you to Jesus. My child, trust in Him. I love you and I will always be with you.

* Michael has received several messages since February 11, 1995. It has been decided, after much prayer, to share some of these messages because from them, we believe, you will receive great graces and a further insight into the call of Our Lord and His Mother. That being:

- placing God at the center of our lives

- fostering a great love for the Blessed Sacrament

- the need for conversion in our own hearts and in the whole world

- love of prayer and sacrifice.

APRIL 15, 1995 - HOLY SATURDAY — I announce today that I will come to you again, very soon, and afterwards on particular days. My child, it gives me great joy to be with you again. I, too, have missed you. I love you , my little one. Again persevere in goodness and help lead others to my Son. Remember what I have said to you and use well the gifts that my Son has given you to help souls come to know and love Him. Go, my little one, and bring this light to others. I love you.

MAY 13, 1995 - FEAST OF OUR LADY OF THE BLESSED SAC-RAMENT — My dear child, stay close to my Immaculate Heart. Persevere in prayer and in living a good and holy life. Be pure, humble, and charitable. Do not allow the subtle snares of the world to lead you away from my Son and me. I am your loving Mother, the Mother of All. I am the Mediatrix of all graces, ... Coredemptrix.

My dear little one, continue to be a soul of prayer and sacrifice. Pray, still, for those intentions which I have confided to you. Love and forgive. Speak only with kind words. Words, my child, that build up not words which tear down. And, as always, love my Son, Jesus, Who is truly with you in the Most Blessed Sacrament of the Altar. Go in peace.

AUGUST 15, 1995 - (JESUS) - (FEAST OF THE ASSUMPTION) - While Michael was praying before the Tabernacle — The great love I have for My children here in the Blessed Sacrament. Speak to them of My love, teach them My love, be an example of My love.

SEPTEMBER 22, 1995 — My dear little one, ... take down my words. I call you to continue to follow my Son with love and humility. I ask you today to begin the practice I called you to some years ago, ... that is, to come and spend fifteen minutes with me to pray and repair for the many sins which cause my motherly heart so much sorrow. This is how I would like you to come in reparation.

On Monday, I ask you to repair, by your love, for all the sins of the flesh; for all the impurity and immorality which daily fills the hearts of those in the world.

On Tuesday, I ask you to repair, by your love, for all the sins against the innocent ones; for abortion and the abuses against all children and innocent youths.

On Wednesday, I call you to repair for the sins of my priest-sons and religious. For those who are in need of the mercy of my Son because of their ingratitude and the darkness which fills their hearts. And also for those priest-sons and religious who, daily, strive to do the Holy Will of God.

On Thursday, I call upon you to come and pray for the Church. Especially, for all bishops, cardinals and my beloved son, the Pope. As well, I call upon you to pray, in a special way, for those struggling to persevere in their faith amidst the trials of their lives.

On Friday, I call upon you to spend fifteen minutes with me for the intentions closest to my heart. On this day, I ask you to meditate, in a special way, on the Passion of my Son.

On Saturday, I call upon you to pray for the sick and suffering, especially for those in their last hour who will die in the hours and days to come.

Finally on Sunday, I ask you to spend those minutes with me thanking my Son, Our Lord, Jesus Christ, for all the goodness of His Heart and all the wonderful things He bestows upon His children.

I call you, my little one, because of the generosity of your love for my Son. I know that you are always willing to say "yes" to the Mother who loves you so. Go in Peace.

Early in the messages, Our Lady asked Michael to spend a certain period of time with her, which Michael did. Our Lady has asked this of him again and now, in a special way, with the break-up of the days and the choosing of different intentions. You are invited, if you wish, to pray for a few moments each day for the given intention that Our Lady requested.

NOVEMBER 7, 1995 - (JESUS) — Will you stay with Me and ease the pains of My heart caused by the intratitude of so many?"

NOVEMBER 14, 1995 - (JESUS) — I am there .. for all. "I am there..." - Our Lord is speaking of His real presence in the Holy Eucharist.

DECEMBER 7, 1995 - EVE OF THE FEAST OF THE IMMACU-LATE CONCEPTION (VISION AND MESSAGE OF OUR LORD AND HIS MOTHER) — Micheal relates, I saw Our Lord in a white tunic with a gold sash around His waist and a red mantle over His shoulders and down around Him. He had a peaceful, but serious look upon His face. He stood before me with His arms at His sides, still, seemingly in an inviting gesture. He said, **"My child, I have come again and again to call My people, to draw them to Me. In these days I come again... and with Me, My Mother, to awaken you from your sleep. Many have listened, they have sought My mercy, but many more have ignored Me."** There was a pause and then He said, **"My child, look upon My heart and see the gift of My love, given to all**..." When He spoke these words, He pointed with both of His hands to His heart, upon which I saw a blazing, white Host (as I had seen in the vision of January of 1993). The Host was in front of His heart. After a moment He continued to speak, "**May you, with those who have also given Me their hearts, continue to make reparation for the souls who remain obstinate in their sin, ... for those, and they are many, who may be eternally lost**." As He said these words, He held His left hand out - flat - palm facing upward and above His hand, in mid-air, was a gold chalice and a Host (the Host was floating in mid-air above the chalice).

After another moment, He stretched out His arms in a sign of His power and said, "**I come to warn the world that it is in great danger ... My hand of Justice must fall to purify it. I am the Alpha and the Omega, the beginning and the end and lo, ... I will return.**"

His voice carried great authority when He said this. I was overcome with my sin and my nothingness before Him. My soul shuddered and I could not bare to look in His direction when He said. "**I am the Alpha and the Omega...**"

After He spoke these words to me, He looked to His right, gesturing with His right arm, and a doorway opened and I saw many scenes concerning possible trials for the world in the future (these events, I understood, are dependent upon our response). After these scenes passed, Our Lady stood in the doorway, her hands folded as in prayer. She was all in white with a shimmering gold outline upon her dress. She was incredibly radiant. Our Lady stood before me for a short time and then she smiled and said, "**Listen to my Son ... love Him.**"

At this the vision ended.

Let us "open our hearts" fully to Jesus Christ, our Lord and Savior, and to His Mother, Mary, our advocate and guide — keeping in mind and heart the words that Our Lord gave to Blessed Faustina:

"Jesus, I trust in You."

MESSAGES FROM THE BLESSED VIRGIN MARY
GIVEN TO MICHAEL MCCOLGAN
ON THE TEN COMMANDMENTS

FEBRUARY 19, 1992 - 1ST COMMANDMENT — My dear children, I love you all. You, my dear little ones, have forgotten about the Commandments. You have turned away from them and those of you that know them ignore them and offend the Lord very much in doing so. My children, in calling you back to the Father, I also call you to follow and practice with love and sincerity the laws of God: the Ten Commandments. Be strong and pray, my children.

Concerning the First Commandment of the Law of the Lord, which is **"I Am The Lord Your God, You Shall Have No Other Gods Beside Me."** My dear children, you offend God and you disobey this Commandment by putting your desires and the objects of your desire above your love and desire for God and His truth. My children, of this day, so much occupies your time other than the Lord. I tell you, return to God. Open your hearts and put God at the center of your hearts. Love God above all else. My children, remember this, all else passes away, only God does not pass away. So much of what you do, my children, is useless and petty because in your pride you have decided for this world and its lures over God and what He desires for you. My dear children, do not be of this world. Live in the love of God and respect Him by your actions and by putting Him above all else.

2ND COMMANDMENT — My dear children, concerning the Second Commandment of the Law of the Lord, which is, **"You Shall Not Take The Name Of The Lord Your God In Vain."** I tell you my little ones, that so many of you use your times of hate and desperation to utter the name of God, instead of using it with love and tenderness and respect. My dear ones, call upon the Father with love, with an open heart, with a wish for Him to strengthen you and to help you. Do not use His name with vile hate or in your times of vice as just a word. The name of my Son is holy and sacred and is to be used to heal and mend, not to break and to tear, not to be uttered in a fashion of sin and of contempt. Use the name of God with Love.

3RD COMMANDMENT — My dear children, concerning the 3rd Commandment of the Law of the Lord, which is, **"Remember To Keep Holy The Sabbath."** My children, I tell you, so many of you do not follow this Commandment and if you do it is not out of love but only in practice. So many of my children offend the heart of my Son in a grave manner because they hold unforgiveness, pride, envy and lust within their hearts when they come to church. My children, I ask you, I beg you, my little ones, to open your hearts with love towards God in all times and especially when you are in the house of the Lord. My children, listen to the words of my Son in the Gospel. Open your hearts to the message He wishes for you to hear and live.

My children, go to Confession frequently because many receive the Lord in the Eucharist sacrilegiously. Many are stained with uncountable sins and with mortal sins and they receive the Lord with their souls in the state of a leper's body. My children, confess your offenses and then come ready and open to receive my Son, Who wishes to clothe you with dazzling garments of holiness. You, my children, offend my Son when you receive Him with your souls in an unclean state. Come to Mass with love, ready and open to greet my Son.

4TH COMMANDMENT — My dear children, concerning the 4th Commandment of the Law of the Lord, which is, **"Respect Your Mother and Father."** My dear children, you have forgotten this Commandment. The world heads toward its ruin because the family has been dispersed. The family has been torn apart because of hatred and sin. Satan has used all his power to do this. My children, you who have turned your heads and your hearts from this Commandment, I call you to love one another, to heal the broken ties of the family, to forgive those who have done you wrong. Children of this world, love and respect your mother and father. They are responsible for you and they are responsible for the care and love for you. Love them even if they do you wrong. Forgive as my Son forgave. Parents, love one another and your children. Respect one another and respect your children. Love them, but also discipline them in love so as to lead them to good morals. This world, in its great sin and darkness, continues to lead countless numbers of your children to commit acts of violence, impurity and evil. Parents, look towards St. Joseph and myself. Pray for the protection of your families and continue to guide your children toward God and a love for His Commandments.

FEBRUARY 21, 1992 - 5TH COMMANDMENT — My dear children, concerning the 5th Commandment of the Law of the Lord, which states, **"You Shall Not Kill."** Oh my children, how you have offended God and how you have pierced my Son's heart and my heart with your actions against this Commandment. My children, I am speaking directly about the grave sin of abortion. My children, do you not realize that a child conceived in the womb is life and it receives a soul from the Father in Heaven? How far you have strayed in allowing this sin to be accepted and practiced. My children, the wrath of God will come in due measure because of this sin. Oh, the countless number of my beloved little ones who have been slaughtered while still in their mother's womb! The Guardian Angels of these children await the justice of God for these babies who have been killed and whose lives have been taken away. My children, open your hearts to me, your Mother. I am crying endless tears because you continue to walk in the darkness of your sin and of your great pride. Your actions, my children, offend God and so I ask you to stop this killing of the innocent. I am calling you out of love and I wish to pour the light of my Son out upon your hearts. I love you.

"God proclaims that he is absolute Lord of the life of man, who is formed in His image and likeness (Genesis 1:26-28). Human life is thus given sacred and inviolable character, which reflects the inviolability of the Creator himself. Precisely for this reason God will severely judge every violation of the commandment 'You Shall Not Kill,' the commandment which is at the basis of all life together in society."

(This entire excerpt is taken from Pope John Paul II's Encyclical Letter; *The Gospel of Life*, paragraph number 53)

"Human life is sacred because from its beginning, it involves the creative action of God, and it remains forever in a special relationship with the Creator, who is its sole end. God alone is the Lord of life from its beginning until its end; no one can, in any circumstance, claim for himself the right to destroy directly an innocent human being."

(Excerpt taken from the *Congregation for the Doctrine of the Faith, Instruction on Respect for Human Life in its Origin and on the Dignity of Procreation - Donum Vitae* (February 22, 1987) found in *The Gospel of Life,* paragraph number 53)

MARCH 4, 1992 - 6TH COMMANDMENT — My dear children, I desire you to do penance and make amendment for your sins. My children, go to Confession.

My dear children, my little ones, concerning the 6th Commandment of the Law of the Lord, which is, **"You Shall Not Commit Adultery."** My children, this also means you shall not commit impure acts. Oh my little ones, so submerged in the sea of sin and of impurity. I call you all to look to Heaven, to decide for God and to pull yourself out of the black sea of impurity with Confession and with the most Holy Rosary.

My children, at this time in the world, impurity has become so widespread. It covers everything and is a firm base of all that is around you. My dear children, turn off your televisions and open your hearts to my Son. Television is the vehicle used by my adversary, Satan, to ensnare and tempt all of you into committing sins of impurity and immorality. My children, your bodies are temples of the most Holy One. He should reign supreme, with love, in your hearts. My dear little ones, purify yourselves with the great love of my Son, Jesus, who wishes you to come back to Him. He is imploring all of you to return to Him and to drink of His mercy, thus cleaning yourself of the filth of the world. My children, turn away from all impurity and all indecency and return to my Son, who awaits you with open arms. I call, especially, the youth to come to me and to immerse themselves in my Immaculate Heart. I will cleanse and protect them with my love. My immaculate light will wipe away all impurity and make of you new shining jewels of purity and of love.

MARCH 16, 1992 - 7TH COMMANDMENT — My dear children, concerning the 7th Commandment of the Law of the Lord, which is, **"You Shall Not Steal."** My dear children, the Father in Heaven calls upon each one of you to be glad for what has been given to you and not to be envious of what another one of your brothers and sisters has. My dear children, He calls you to not take anything that you do not have because you are envious and are not pleased and do not accept your gifts. My children, by stealing something from another person you insult the Father in Heaven, Who has given you what you need. Be glad for what your Father in Heaven has given to you. My children, open your hearts and meditate on the gifts of God. My children, be thankful.

8TH COMMANDMENT — My dear children, concerning the 8th Commandment of the Law of the Lord, which is, **"You shall Not Bear False Witness Against Your Neighbor."** My dear little ones, in your world of today many lie and cheat one another to get ahead and to gain profit. This is sinful and detestable in the eyes of the Lord. My children, simply, the Father calls all of you to be truthful and to love all of your brothers and sisters and not to lie against them for your own good or because of your faults or the faults or good of another. My children, the Father in Heaven calls on you to live in the truth.

9TH AND 10TH COMMANDMENTS — My dear children, concerning the 9th and 10th Commandments of the Law of the Lord, which are **"You Shall Not Covet Your Neighbors' House, Or His Wife, Or Any Of His Goods, ... Nothing Of Your Neighbors Shall You Be In Want Of ..."** My dear children, your sinful world of today is in great darkness concerning these Commandments. Many of you, my children, continue to contaminate these ideals and live against these Commandments. My dear children, many of you sin against these Commandments through your blindness. So many of my children cheat and lie in wait for another's goods, ... especially my children, for the wife of another. Because of this sin many marriages have been separated and the children of these marriages have been led into the den of hate and sin, into the den of sorrow and iniquity, because of the actions of those around them.

My children, again, I, your Mother, call you to meditate on the Commandments of the Lord and to incorporate them into your daily actions. My children, I call you to live the Commandments of the Law of the Lord to the letter and to love the Lord above the ways of the world. My children, the Father in Heaven has given the Commandments to you so that you may have a sure guide to salvation and to happiness and peace in your lives. My children, live and love the Commandments of your God. I love you all and I am with you.

OPEN YOUR HEARTS

THE HOLY ROSARY

Begin by making the Sign of the Cross.

Then on the Cross (of the Rosary) say the Apostles' Creed

On the first bead, from the Cross, the Our Father.

On the next 3 beads, 3 Hail Marys for the virtues of Faith, Hope, and Charity.

On the final bead before the center medal, 1 Glory Be.

On the medal mention the first Mystery, meditate on it and say 1 Our Father, then on the following 10 beads say 10 Hail Marys while meditating on the Mystery.

At the end of the 10 Hail Marys, say 1 Glory Be and then the Fatima Prayer.

Then on the spaced bead mention the 2nd Mystery and say 1 Our Father, etc.

Do this until you have done all 5 decades of the set of Mysteries that you are praying. (Going once around the beads)

Then say 1 Hail Holy Queen and the Let Us Pray prayer.

THE MYSTERIES OF THE ROSARY

The Joyful Mysteries
1. The Annunciation
2. The Visitation
3. The Nativity
4. The Presentation in the Temple
5. The Finding of Our Lord in the Temple

The Sorrowful Mysteries
1. The Agony in the Garden
2. The Scourging at the Pillar
3. The Crowning with Thorns
4. The Carrying of the Cross
5. The Crucifixion

The Glorious Mysteries

1. The Resurrection
2. The Ascension into Heaven
3. The Descent of the Holy Spirit
4. The Assumption
5. The Coronation of the Blessed Virgin

THE CREED

I believe in God, the Father Almighty, Creator of Heaven and Earth; and in Jesus Christ, His only Son, Our Lord; Who was conceived by the Holy Spirit, born of the Virgin Mary, suffered under Pontius Pilate, was crucified; died, and was buried. He descended into Hell; the third day He arose again from the dead; He ascended into Heaven, sitteth at the right hand of God the Father Almighty; from thence He shall come to judge the living and the dead. I believe in the Holy Spirit, the Holy Catholic Church, the communion of Saints, the forgiveness of sins, the resurrection of the body, and life everlasting. Amen.

OUR FATHER

Our Father, Who art in Heaven, hallowed be Thy name, Thy Kingdom come, Thy Will be done, on earth as it is in Heaven. Give us this day, our daily bread, and forgive us our trespasses, as we forgive those who trespass against us, and lead us not into temptation, but deliver us from evil. Amen.

HAIL MARY

Hail Mary, full of grace, the Lord is with thee. Blessed art thou among women and blessed is the fruit of thy womb, Jesus. Holy Mary, Mother of God, pray for us sinners, now, and at the hour of our death. Amen.

GLORY BE

Glory be to the Father, and to the Son, and to the Holy Spirit. As it was in the beginning, is now, and ever shall be, world without end. Amen.

FATIMA PRAYER

O my Jesus, forgive us our sins, save us from the eternal fires of Hell and lead all souls into Heaven especially those in most need of Thy mercy. Amen.

HAIL HOLY QUEEN

Hail, Holy Queen, Mother of Mercy, our life, our sweetness, and our hope! To thee do we cry, poor banished children of Eve; to thee do we send up our sighs, mourning and weeping in this valley of tears. Turn, then, most gracious Advocate, thine eyes of mercy towards us; and after this our exile show unto us the Blessed Fruit of thy womb, Jesus; O clement, o loving, O sweet Virgin Mary.

Pray for us, O Holy Mother of God, that we may be made worthy of the promises of Christ.

LET US PRAY

O God, Whose only begotten Son, by His life, death and resurrection, has purchased for us the rewards of eternal life, grant, we beseech Thee, that while meditating upon these mysteries of the Most Holy Rosary of the Blessed Virgin Mary, we may imitate what they contain, and obtain what they promise; through the same Christ Our Lord. Amen.

THE DIVINE MERCY CHAPLET

(To be said on the Rosary)
1 Our Father
1 Hail Mary
I Believe In God (the Creed)

then on the OUR FATHER BEADS you will say the following words:
ETERNAL FATHER, I OFFER YOU THE BODY AND BLOOD, SOUL AND DIVINITY OF YOUR DEARLY BELOVED SON, OUR LORD, JESUS CHRIST, IN ATONEMENT FOR OUR SINS AND THOSE OF THE WHOLE WORLD.

then, on the HAIL MARY BEADS you will say the following words:
FOR THE SAKE OF HIS SORROWFUL PASSION HAVE MERCY
ON US AND ON THE WHOLE WORLD.
then,
in conclusion THREE TIMES you will recite these words:
HOLY GOD, HOLY MIGHTY ONE, HOLY IMMORTAL ONE,
HAVE MERCY ON US AND ON THE WHOLE WORLD.
then,
JESUS, I TRUST IN YOU.

THE CHAPLET OF TRUTH

(To be said on the Rosary)
Apostles' Creed
One Our Father
Three Hail Marys
One Glory Be
On The Our Father Beads
Father in heaven, protect the true and infallible Church of which your
Son is Lord and King. Protect the faithful and strengthen and fill with
grace your servants within the Church, the priests and religious. Father
in Heaven, give wisdom in grace to the Holy Father and to the bishops.
Protect and guide, always, Your Church Militant, Suffering, Triumphant.
On the Hail Mary Beads
Father, Son, and Holy Spirit, Triune God, pour out upon the Church
divine grace, so that it may continue to unify the faithful and teach
upon the earth the words of Our Lord and Savior, Jesus Christ, Re-
deemer of Mankind.
Three Hail Marys
One Hail Holy Queen
One Glory Be

* For the full explanation of the Chaplet of Truth see message of February 15, 1993.

THE MEMORARE

Remember, O most gracious Virgin Mary, that never was it known that
anyone who fled to thy protection, implored thy help, or sought thy

intercession, was left unaided. Inspired with this confidence, I fly unto thee, O Virgin of virgins, my Mother. To Thee I come, before thee I stand, sinful and sorrowful. O Mother of the Word Incarnate, despise not my petitions, but, in thy mercy, hear and answer me. Amen.

PRAYER TO SAINT MICHAEL

St. Michael, the Archangel, defend us in battle, be our safeguard against the wickedness and snares of the devil. May God rebuke him we humbly pray, and do you, prince of the heavenly host, by the power of God, cast into Hell Satan and all the evil spirits, who roam through the world seeking the ruin of souls. Amen.

EUCHARISTIC PRAYER OF AKITA

Most Sacred Heart of Jesus, TRULY present in the Holy Eucharist, I consecrate my body and soul to be entirely one with Your Heart, being sacrificed at every instant on all altars of the world and giving praise to the Father, pleading for the coming of His Kingdom.

Please receive this humble offering of myself. Use me as You will for the glory of the Father and the salvation of souls.

Most Holy Mother of God, never let me be separated from Your Divine Son. Please defend and protect me as Your special child. Amen.

ACT OF CONSECRATION
TO THE IMMACULATE HEART OF MARY
For Parishes, Families, and Individuals

O Immaculate Heart of Mary, Queen of Heaven and earth and tender Mother of men, in accordance with your ardent wish made known at Fatima I consecrate to you myself, my brethren, my country and the whole human race.

Reign over us and teach us how to make the heart of Jesus reign and triumph in us and around us as it has reigned and triumphed in you.

Reign over us, dearest Mother, that we may be yours in prosperity and in adversity, in joy and in sorrow, in health and in sickness, in life and in death. O most compassionate heart of Mary, Queen of Virgins, watch over our minds and hearts and preserve them from the deluge of impurity which you didst lament so sorrowfully at Fatima. We want to be pure like you. We want to atone for the many sins committed against

Jesus and you. We want to call down upon our country and the whole world the peace of God in justice and charity.

Therefore, we now promise to imitate your virtues by the practice of a Christian life and we resolve to offer you five decades of the Rosary each day together with our sacrifices in a spirit of reparation and penance. Amen.

PRAYER TO THE ETERNAL HIGH PRIEST

O Jesus, Eternal Priest, keep Your priests within the shelter of Your Most Sacred Heart, where none can touch them. Keep unstained their annointed hands, which daily touch Your Sacred Body. Keep unsullied their lips, daily tinged with Your Precious Blood. Keep pure and unworldly their hearts, sealed with the sublime mask of the Priesthood. Let Your Holy Love surround and protect them from the world's contagion. Bless their labors with abundant fruit, and may the souls to whom they minister be their joy and consolation here, and their everlasting crown in the hereafter. Amen

(St. Therese of the Child Jesus)

LABORERS FOR THE HARVEST

O Jesus, Good Shepherd, raise up in all parish communities priests and deacons, religious, consecrated lay people, and missionaries according to the needs of the whole world, which You love and want to save. Guide the steps of those who have generously welcomed Your call and are preparing themselves for Holy Orders of the Profession of the Evangelical Councils.

Direct Your loving gaze to the many well-disposed young people and invite them to follow You. Help them to understand that only in you can they achieve their fulfillment. We entrust these great desires of Your Heart to the powerful intercession of Mary, Mother and model of all vocations, and beg You to sustain our faith in the certainty that the Father will listen to what You Yourself have instructed us to ask for. Amen.

(Mt. 9:38) (Pope John Paul II)